the Gardener's Guide to Water Gardening

INTRODUCTION

Last summer I was lucky enough to have a spare weekend (something of a rarity in my life) when I could attend some of the events going on in the village I live in. Faldingworth is a small rural village in Lincolnshire, England, which holds a weekend festival every summer. Similar events are held in many villages throughout the country and I dare say throughout much of Europe and America. Craft stalls, dancing in the village hall, treasure hunts, etc.

One thing which my village has introduced throughout the weekend is the opening of gardens, by those who wish to do so, to public view. These are not the great house gardens you often see on television but family gardens created and loved by gardeners the world over. What struck me as so surprising was the number of people who had lovely garden ponds. I had never realized just how many one little village could contain. Many of these had been integrated into the garden and were as much a water garden as a fish pond.

This book has been written for those people who are primarily gardeners who want to include a pond in their garden but are a little unsure how to go about it. Fish and all the other animals and wildlife which accompany a pond have been included, as well as the basics of making a pond. The emphasis in this book is on the plants and other aspects of water gardening which will be of most interest to a gardener. I hope the reader will forgive this bias and enjoy reading about a side of pond keeping which is often neglected in other books. Indeed, even if you are not a keen gardener at the moment, hopefully this book will spark some interest in the subject and expand your hobby from fish keeping to water gardening in all its forms.

WHAT ARE QUARTERLIES?

Books, the usual way information of this sort is transmitted, can be too slow. Sometimes by the time a book is written and published, the material contained therein is a year or two old...and no new material has been added during that time. Only a book in a magazine form can bring breaking stories and current information. A magazine is streamlined in production, so we have adopted certain magazine publishing techniques in the creation of this Garden Pond Quarterly. Magazines also can be much cheaper than books because they are supported by advertising. To combine these assets into a great publication, we are issuing this Quarterly in both magazine and book format at different prices.

Garden Ponds Quarterly

yearBOOKS, INC.
Dr. Herbert R. Axelrod,
Founder & Chairman

Dominique DeVito
Chief Editor

yearBOOKS are all photo composed, color separated and designed on Scitex equipment in Neptune, N.J. with the following staff:

DIGITAL PRE-PRESS
Patricia Northrup
Supervisor

Robert Onyrscuk
Jose Reyes

COMPUTER ART
Patti Escabi
Sandra Taylor Gale
Candida Moreira
Joanne Muzyka
Francine Shulman

ADVERTISING SALES
Nancy S. Rivadeneira
Advertising Sales Director
Cheryl J. Blyth
Advertising Account Manager
Amy Manning
Advertising Director
Sandy Cutillo
Advertising Coordinator

©yearBOOKS, Inc.
1 TFH Plaza
Neptune, N.J. 07753
Completely manufactured in
Neptune, N.J.   USA

Design by Candida Moreira
Cover design by Sherise Buhagiar

CONTENTS

When I created my first pond many years ago it was essentially just a fish pond with a water lily and a few bunches of oxygenating plants in it. The main focus of this and most of my subsequent ponds was the fish, not the plants. Indeed it was not until I moved to my present house that I finally developed a keen interest in water gardening in all its forms.

This interest started not with the plants themselves but Newts. A breeding colony of endangered Great Crested Newts to be precise. The farmer behind our property started to fill in the last part of a natural pond which contained the only breeding colony of these lovely creatures in my area, so as he was filling in his pond I was digging out mine. Since amphibians need easy access into and out of a pond, I decided to create a bog area around three sides of the pond and make a natural progression from water to dry land.

This opened up a huge range of plants to me which I had never been able to keep before and I was soon hooked on collecting more and more of them. Some proved to be an absolute menace by spreading uncontrollably throughout the whole area and threatening to strangle all the more delicate and, in many cases, more beautiful plants. Others were not so aggressive but just looked like a clump of dry grass. Eventually I settled on those I liked and weeded out the others I thought totally unsuitable for my small pond.

Just as things were settling down and growing nicely I noticed a few new species of bog plants coming on the market and I had to try them. The next year even more new ones appeared and more are still popping up all the time. The reason behind this sudden increase in the range of plants is the increasing popularity of pond keeping. Not too long ago I had to visit a specialist aquarium shop to buy a pond liner and some other aquatic equipment. The era of aquatic gardening has finally come of age, and aquarium shops are responding.

LOCATION 5

DESIGNING A POND 9

CONSTRUCTING A POND 13

WATER FEATURES ... 19

FILTRATION & POND MAINTENANCE ... 27

SUITABLE BOG PLANTS ... 49

AQUATIC PLANTS ... 31

A ROCKERY BY YOUR POND ... 59

THE BOG GARDEN ... 39

FISH ... 62

Distributed in the UNITED STATES to the Pet Trade by T.F.H. Publications, Inc., One T.F.H. Plaza, Neptune City, NJ 07753; on the Internet at www.tfh.com; in CANADA Rolf C. Hagen Inc., 3225 Sartelon St. Laurent-Montreal Quebec H4R 1E8; Pet Trade by H & L Pet Supplies Inc., 27 Kingston Crescent, Kitchener, Ontario N2B 2T6; in ENGLAND by T.F.H. Publications, PO Box 15, Waterlooville PO7 6BQ; in AUSTRALIA AND THE SOUTH PACIFIC by T.F.H. (Australia), Pty. Ltd., Box 149, Brookvale 2100 N.S.W., Australia; in NEW ZEALAND by Brooklands Aquarium Ltd. 5 McGiven Drive, New Plymouth, RD1 New Zealand; in SOUTH AFRICA, Rolf C. Hagen S.A. (PTY.) LTD. P.O. Box 201199, Durban North 4016, South Africa; in Japan by T.F.H. Publications, Japan—Jiro Tsuda, 10-12-3 Ohjidai, Sakura, Chiba 285, Japan. Published by T.F.H. Publications, Inc.

MANUFACTURED IN THE
UNITED STATES OF AMERICA
BY T.F.H. PUBLICATIONS, INC.

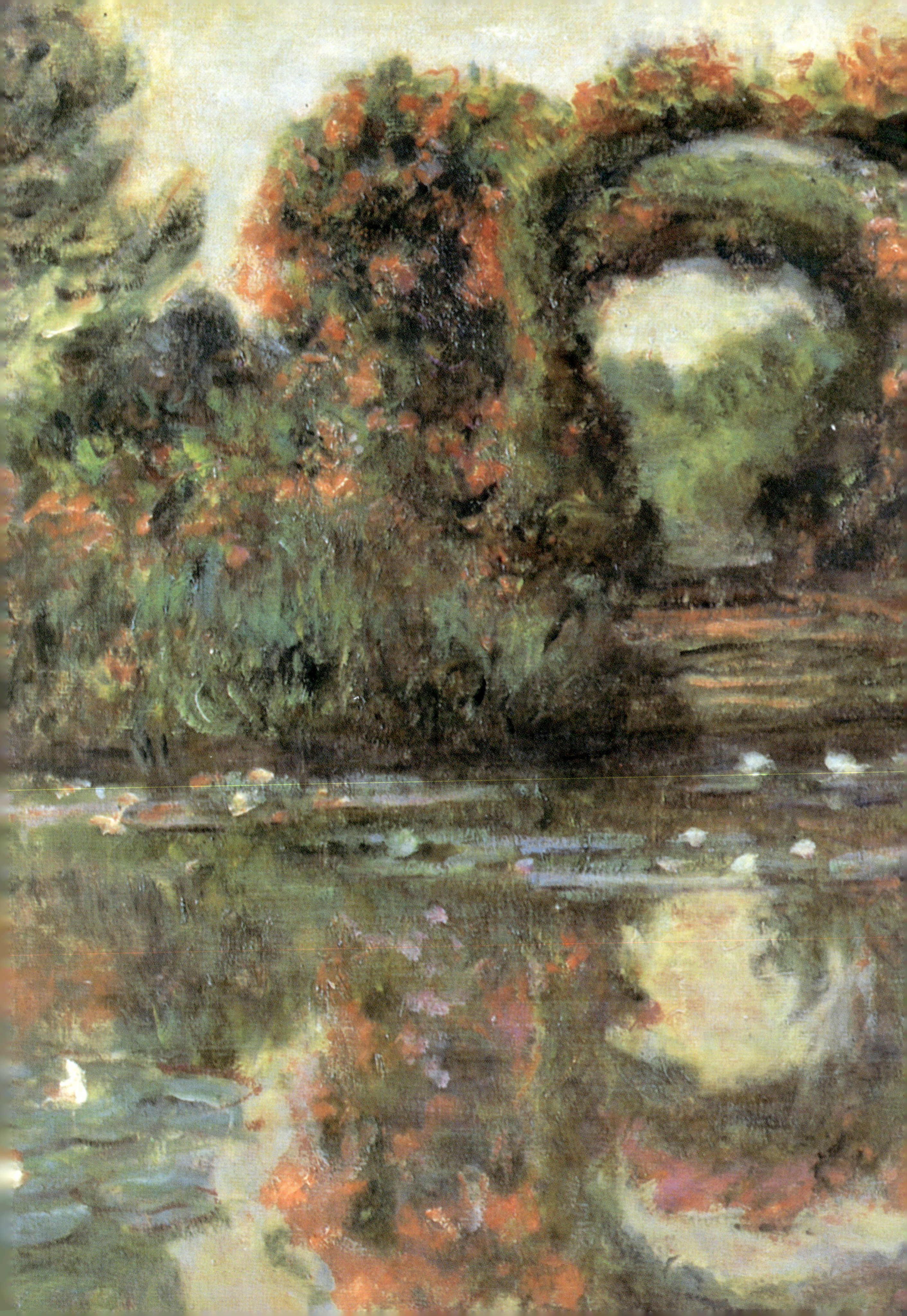

LOCATION

location

The chapter openings feature Monet's *Water Lilies* paintings because every water gardening book should be dedicated to him. He made more paintings, and more FAMOUS and VALUABLE paintings than all the other great artists combined. Using the same lily pond, Monet painted during all hours of the day and all seasons of the year. His lily pond paintings are to be found in major art museums worldwide.

For most gardeners the proper location for a pond will be where it looks best. The problem with this is it may well be completely the wrong place for the health and well being of the plants and animals which will be living in it. Lilies and many other pond plants and marginals love to be out in full sun. If you think a pond would look perfect in that shady corner of the garden next to the wall and under overhanging trees, then very few of the plants will do well. Indeed, if the wrong trees overhang it, then they may shed poisonous leaves or fruit into the water. These may pollute the water and kill your fish.

I remember one pond I constructed too close to a fig tree. The large leaves were easy enough to remove from the water but some overripe figs, falling off the tree into the water one summer, soon started to rot and polluted the water. Within a few days the water turned gray and all the fish died. So out in the open and well clear of trees is where you need to position your pond if at all possible.

Fruit trees are not the only hazard for a pond when it comes to home grown produce. Many gardeners have a vegetable plot or at least a few fruit bushes in the garden. To keep these pest free some people regularly spray with chemicals of one sort or another. Almost all these sprays are deadly poisonous to fish and have to be kept well clear of your pond. Don't forget your neighbor's activities as well. When plants are being sprayed some of the chemical will drift away in the wind and settle a long way from the point of origin. It is no good complaining that all your fish have died because your neighbor sprayed his vegetables and you placed your pond close to his plot.

Another factor to consider when working out where to place your pond is safety. Ask yourself if children or elderly people use that part of the garden. A pond is lovely to look at but it can be a real hazard to a child or elderly person if they fall in. In these circumstances make sure you fence it off or place it in another part of the garden.

Another factor to take into consideration is how far away are any services you need. If you are planning to have a fountain, filter or special lighting in your pond then you will have to arrange for electricity to be available. This will mean digging a trench from the house to the pond in which the wire can be buried.

A source of water will also be needed. In most cases a hose long enough to reach from the tap right into the pond can be purchased without too much trouble. Make sure you measure the distance out before you buy the hose otherwise you could do what I did. Last time I built a pond I found the hose was just a foot short of the pond's edge. The only way I could fill the pond was by standing there with the hose held in my hand, hour after hour, spraying water upwards into the air so it would land in the pond.

Another important factor, which so often is forgotten when thinking about a pond, is a path. An attractive pond draws people to it like bees 'round a honey pot. One of the houses in my village has a pond about 20 feet to the right of the path going up to the front door. If you watch visitors arriving at the house, almost every one of them makes a detour to have a look at the pond. If no path had been included in its design,

location

Water gardens are so popular because they readily adapt to existing conditions. For most water gardeners, the best location for a pond is where it looks best.

location

the grass would soon be worn away by tramping feet.

The next thing to consider is how exposed the site is. A pond exposed to winter's chill winds will be much colder than one in a more sheltered position. Walls or solid fences tend to make winds eddy and swirl around which may cause problems in other parts of the garden. In fact a hedge or shrubs slow down and break up the wind much better than any solid windbreak. In a formal garden it is worth surrounding the pond with a hedge positioned far enough away so as not to cast a shadow but close enough to shield the pond from the wind's effect. In an informal setting shrubs are more suitable. Once again, they should be planted close enough for their effect to be felt but not too close so they cast a shadow on the pond or their leaves fall into the water.

If you have a water-logged hollow you may be forgiven for thinking this is the natural site for a pond and to a certain extent you would be right. Ponds tend to look more natural when they are tucked away in a hollow but the problem with this sort of site is that when you dig a hole it fills with water. Hey, presto! A natural pond, I hear you shout. Well for a time maybe, but during the first long dry spell the water will dry up and your fish and plants will be left high and dry. Trying to build a concrete pond in such conditions is almost impossible and if you install a liner then there is a great risk of water collecting in the hole and causing the liner to float away from the base and sides. No, this sort of location has to be scrubbed off the list of possible sites.

Once you have sorted out the location you can start to think about the design of your pond.

Photo by Michael Gilroy.

Water gardens must be fenced in or surrounded with heavy foliage to prevent the accidental drowning of the young, the elderly and animals.

DESIGNING A POND

designing a pond

SIZE & SHAPE

The first thing to decide when designing your pond is how big it is going to be. In many things in the garden you try out an idea on a small scale first before moving on to a large version. With ponds this can lead to a disaster. For many different reasons a large pond produces much better results than a small one. So my advice is to start with as large a construction as possible bearing in mind the size of the site and the cost of the materials.

If you are limited on space or money, try not to go below a size of 50 sq. ft. of water surface area. This may sound like a large pond but in fact it is only slightly larger than a 7 ft. square. To give yourself a better idea of how big this is, measure it out on the ground using a hose or rope. Stand back and look at it in the context of the whole garden. If it looks too small increase it until it looks in scale with its surroundings.

Once you have worked out how big your pond will be you need to decide on the actual shape. If you have a very formal garden then chances are you will want a formal pond as well. Squares, rectangles, ovals and circles all look good in this sort of setting. If you would like some statues associated with the pond (or in it) then try to buy them before the pond is constructed. This way you can work them into the design and produce a cohesive whole.

Informal ponds can be any shape you like but steer clear of very complicated shapes. They can be a nightmare to construct and rarely look as good in real life as you think they will. For some strange reason a kidney shape tends to be the most natural looking. Of the prefabricated ponds more of this shape are sold than any other.

When working out the design you can again use the hose or rope to lay the design out on the ground. If a bog garden or a rock garden is going to be included in the design, mark these areas off as well. When you think it looks right move well away and look at it from all parts of the garden. If you will be able to see it from the house, have a look from an upstairs window. A little thought at this stage will help you produce a thing of beauty rather than just a hole in the ground.

DEPTH

Just how deep to make your pond will depend to a certain extent on the weather conditions prevalent in your area. At least some of the pond will have to be deep enough to prevent the water from freezing solid in the winter. If you live in Florida where a frost is rare, let alone ice, then this need not be a factor. In the U.K. and for many areas of the temperate world, freezing conditions will be experienced for at least part of the winter. Indeed, as I write this, my pond is frozen over and has been for the last week.

CONSTRUCTION

Originally there was basically one choice when it came to building a pond - concrete. It was possible to build a pond out of clay but this is a very skilled process which more often than not led to disaster. Even using concrete it was a very laborious process which, unless you got it just right, could still lead to a leaking pond.

Today, however, we have a few more choices. Prefabricated ponds come in fiberglass and heavy duty plastic. Plastic is cheapest but does not last so long and can be

---

The popularity of water gardening has prompted the manufacture of CD-Rom materials that provide how-to instructions and color photos that cover a wide range of water gardening issues. For a pet shop nearest you call (530) 872-1013. Photo courtesy of Nature Zone.

designing a pond

Patti and David Rutledge, America's largest growers of aquatic plants (doing business as Horizon Growers, Ramona, Ca 92065; fax (760)789-0297) still enjoy an outdoor water garden into which they drain their farm when it rains.

The Dusit Rayavadee Resort in Krabi, Thailand features a lovely water garden in front of each bungalow.

rather fragile. Fiberglass is much more durable and is a good option if you want a quick, easy and reliable pond. Its only drawback is that you have to have one in the shape it is sold in. Despite this drawback they were the most popular way of making a garden pond.

Liners started to come in about the time I first dug a pond. Initially they were made of heavy duty polyethylene sheeting which breaks down rather quickly in sunlight. Hiding the edges under stone paving helped reduce this problem but it was still a major drawback to this type of pond.

P.V.C. and synthetic rubber liners were next on the scene. These are much more durable and are now the most popular way of making a pond.

Laminated P.V.C. has a proven life span of up to 15 years and is cheaper than butyl rubber. Butyl rubber, however, lasts much longer (some estimates put its working life at 100 years) and is more durable and less prone to puncture than P.V.C. In my opinion this is the material to go for if you can afford it. Pet shops usually carry several kinds of liners, or they can order them for you.

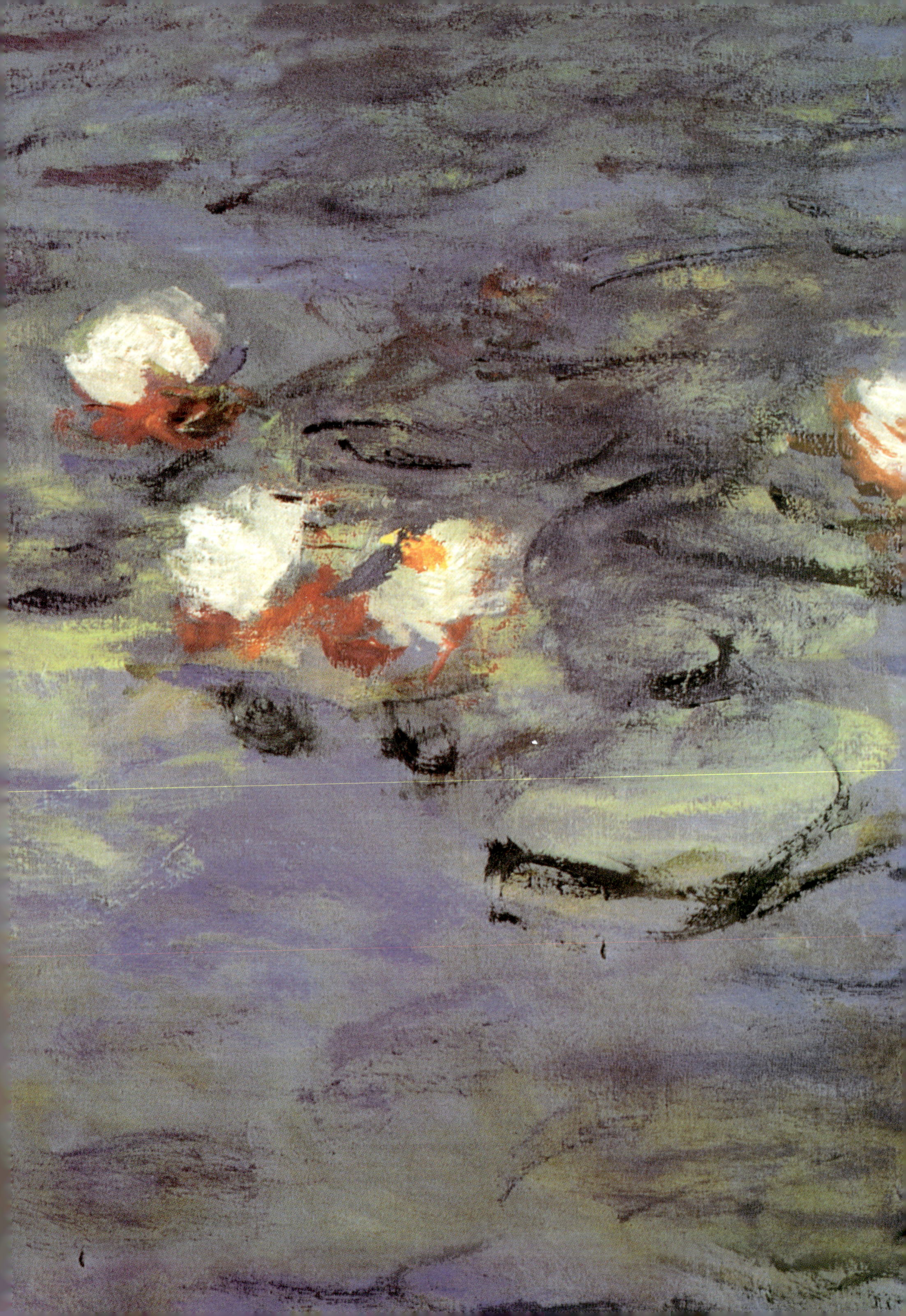

CONSTRUCTING A POND

constructing a pond

CONCRETE

Personally I would like to consign concrete, as a substance to build ponds with, to the history books where it now belongs. Some people do, however, still want to use it to construct their pond, so for completeness I am including a section on how to do this. If you end up with a bad back, leaky pond and something which looks like a refugee from a badly constructed 1960's housing estate, don't blame me! Being fair about it, though, properly constructed and once weathered for a year or two, a concrete pond can look good and will serve its purpose for many years to come.

To construct a successful concrete pond you must make sure you have everything in hand before you start the job. It can spell real trouble if you run out of concrete before the job is finished, so make sure you have enough of everything to complete the whole thing and that means time as well as material.

The first thing is to dig out the hole. This involves a lot of very hard work (particularly if you have a heavy clay soil) and if the pond is large it is a good idea to hire a mechanical digger for the day to do the job for you. Alternatively call in a few debts people owe you and blackmail them into helping. If you know some real suckers you can have a "Pond Digging Party" and invite them over to help dig the pond. Combined with plenty of drink and some nice food they may eventually forgive you.

Whatever method you employ, the walls should slope outwards 20 degrees from the vertical and the hole must be 5" larger all round and 10" deeper than the planned pond size. The top must also be level. Use a spirit level resting on a long piece of wood to check this. Next place hardcore over the bottom to a depth of 5" and ram it into place. This hardcore should be made up of a mixture of broken bricks, stones and coarse gravel and forms the foundation for your pond. It is a good idea to ram some of this into the walls as well.

Now you need to make shuttering to hold the concrete in place while it is drying. This needs to be 5" smaller than the hole and follow the walls' contours. Don't forget the 20 degree slope and include any shelves you want for baskets containing marginals. Use chipboard cladding for straight walls and bent hardboard for curved ones. Making this shuttering for a square or rectangular pond is relatively easy but it can be an absolute nightmare for more intricate shapes.

Once your shuttering and hole are ready you can work out how much concrete you are going to need and make sure you have enough of the ingredients to make it. The way to work this out is to measure the surface area of the base, sides and shelves. For every 10 sq ft. of this you are going to need 56 pounds of cement, 112 lbs. of sharp sand, 224 lbs. of coarse aggregate and $1 \frac{1}{4}$ lb. of waterproofing powder. The waterproofing powder should be mixed into the cement before you start mixing the ingredients together by volume.

To mix the concrete use a bucket to measure out the dry ingredients as follows : 3 parts aggregate to 2 parts sharp sand and 1 part of cement (with waterproofing powder). Put these into a

A four-foot pre-cast pond set up and photographed by Rich Sacher.

constructing a pond

Photo by Michael Gilroy.

A pre-formed liner, made to look like stone, in a very formal setting.

mixer and make sure they are thoroughly mixed before adding water to make them into a stiff paste which will hold its shape when cut with the shovel.

Spread this on the base to a depth of 2" and then add a layer of chicken wire or reinforcing mesh before putting another 2" layer over the top. The should now be left to dry for an hour. In hot weather only leave it half an hour before installing the shuttering. Now the walls can be formed by filling the space between the shuttering and hole with concrete. This is where at least one other person is a great help, because as one mix is being used another can be prepared.

When the walls are complete leave the pond for a day or two before adding the rendering. This needs to be done when the concrete is firm enough to work but not too dry. If the weather is hot use wet sacking over the bottom and walls to slow down the drying process.

To form the rendering use 1 part cement (to which waterproofing powder has been added at the rate of 5 lb per cwt.) to 3 parts sharp sand. Once again mix the ingredients dry before adding water to make a stiff paste. This is then trowelled onto the walls and base 1" thick. Once it has dried out you can either paint sealant over the concrete to seal in the poisonous free lime or you can start the washing process. To do this fill the pond with water and leave it for a week. Empty it out and scrub round with a stiff brush. Refill the pond and leave it for another week before repeating the process again. In all do this 4 to 6 times before permanently filling the pond.

If you can afford it, hire a mason who specializes in swimming pools to make a garden pond for you.

PREFABRICATED

Prefabricated ponds are by far and away the easiest sort of pond to install. First of all, dig the hole slightly larger all round than the pond but only as deep as the maximum depth. Remove any large or sharp stones from the walls and base. Then position the pond and check it is sitting in the hole perfectly level. Use a spirit level resting on a long piece of wood to do this. Now back fill until all the shelves and the upper lip are supported by soil. One final check with the spirit level and you can now position edging stones or turf to disguise the edge and fill with water. If the soil does not support the plastic pond, it will crack when filled with water.

LINER PONDS

These are almost as easy to install as a prefabricated pond. First of all remove a couple of inches of soil from the pond's area and for several feet around. Check that this area is level using a spirit level resting on a long piece of wood. Now dig the hole to the correct size and shape you have already decided upon. The soil taken out of the hole should be moved well clear of the hole but not too far if you are going to use it to build a rockery or waterfall. The walls must slope outwards by a 20 degree angle from the vertical. Make sure you incorporate any marginal shelves or bog garden area you want and

constructing a pond

Drawings by Jan Balon.

1 Use a flexible garden hose to shape your proposed water garden.

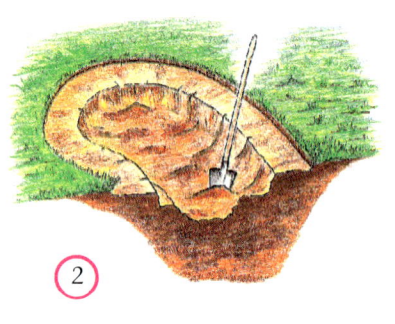

2 Dig around the hose in a shallow manner to make the ledge then dig out the center.

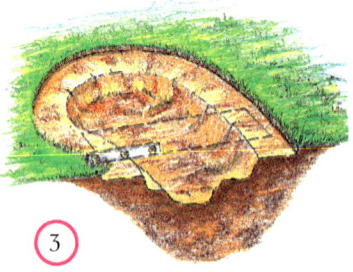

3 Use a flat panel of wood, fiberglass, glass or anything which doesn't bend and be sure that the pool is level, otherwise the water will flow out of the pool at the low end.

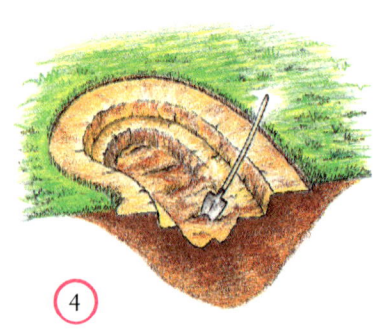

4 Make terraces for planters at varying depths.

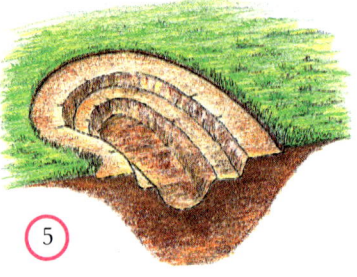

5 When you have finished digging, be sure that all of the dirt is firmly packed and parallel to the surfaces at the edge of the pond.

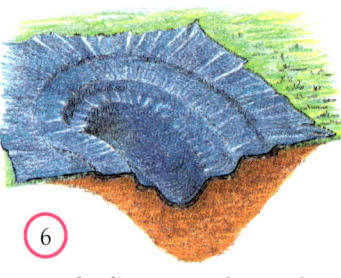

6 Drape the liner over the pool you have dug, being sure that you have enough liner to cover the inside of the pool once water has been added.

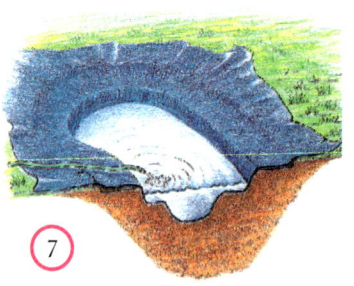

7 Add water SLOWLY. Warm water is better as it will make the liner more flexible as it fills.

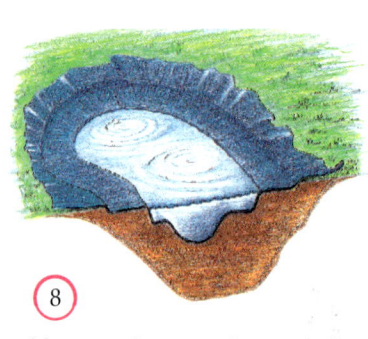

8 Add water almost to the top ledge. A few inches will evaporate as the water ages before you add fishes or plants.

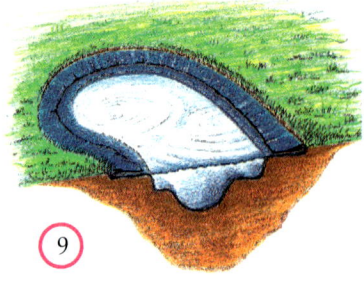

9 Trim off the excess liner leaving a 6 inch wide flap all around. Fold the flap over preparatory to adding stones along the edge of the pond.

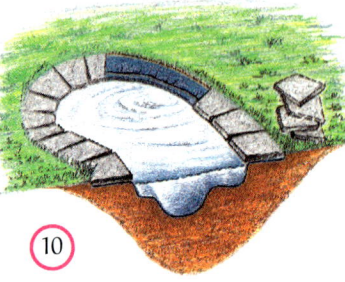

10 Lay a foundation of light cement and place the paving stones in position, but lay all the stones in position BEFORE you cement them in place in case they don't fit around the pond properly.

11 Allow the water and pond to settle and the paving stones to firmly bond into the cement.

12 Once all the air bubbles have left the sides of the pond and the water turns milky, then green, it is safe to add fishes and plants. You can also add decorations both inside and alongside the pond.

constructing a pond

that all sharp stones or other objects which might puncture the liner are removed.

Now measure the overall length and width of the hole. This is the smallest rectangle that the pond will fit into, not the longest length and width measurements. If a bog garden is being included as an integral part of the pond include this in the measurements as well. To work out the liner size you are going to need to line your pond, add twice the pond's maximum depth to the length and width. So a pond 10 ft. by 6 ft. and 3 ft. deep will need a liner 16 ft. by 12 ft..

If money is at a premium, you may want to buy a liner of a specific size and then work out how big the pond can be from this. Say you can only afford to buy a 15 ft. by 10 ft. liner and you want your pond to be 2 ft. 6 inches at its deepest. By subtracting double the depth we can see your pond will have to fit into a 10 ft. by 5 ft. rectangle.

Once you have your liner, cover the holes, floor and shelves with something to create a smooth, even base. Sand, peat, old newspapers, bits of carpet or underfelt padding will all do the job. If you have very stony soil, you may have to line the walls as well. The top edge must also be lined. Now drape the liner over the hole and fix it round the edges with some heavy flat stones. Pieces of paving are ideal for this. These must be positioned so they weight the liner edge and yet are well clear of the hole.

You are now ready to fill your pond. This will take some time during which you will have to watch things carefully, so make sure you start it early enough in the day. As the liner fills with water it will sag and drop down to the bottom of the hole. Gradually it will stretch out into all the curves and contours of the hole. As the pond fills you can remove some of the weights so that the liner gradually slips into the hole but do this slowly and only when the pond is well over half full.

Once the pond is full, remove the rest of the weights and trim off the surplus liner leaving a 6 inch wide flap all round. To finish off the edge, bed paving stones on 1 part cement to 3 parts sand. These should have a 2 inch lip overhanging the pond. If your pond is going to house amphibians, then at least part of the edge must be made so that they can enter and leave easily. To do this, turf can be used to cover the liner or it can be buried in the soil and plants grown over the edge providing easy access to the pond. Either of these options looks good for the area around a bog garden.

> **If you design a round pond, you will probably need professional assistance. Round concrete ponds are very difficult to build but they can provide a very pleasing effect if tastefully planted and stocked.**

Photo by Dr. Herbert R. Axelrod.

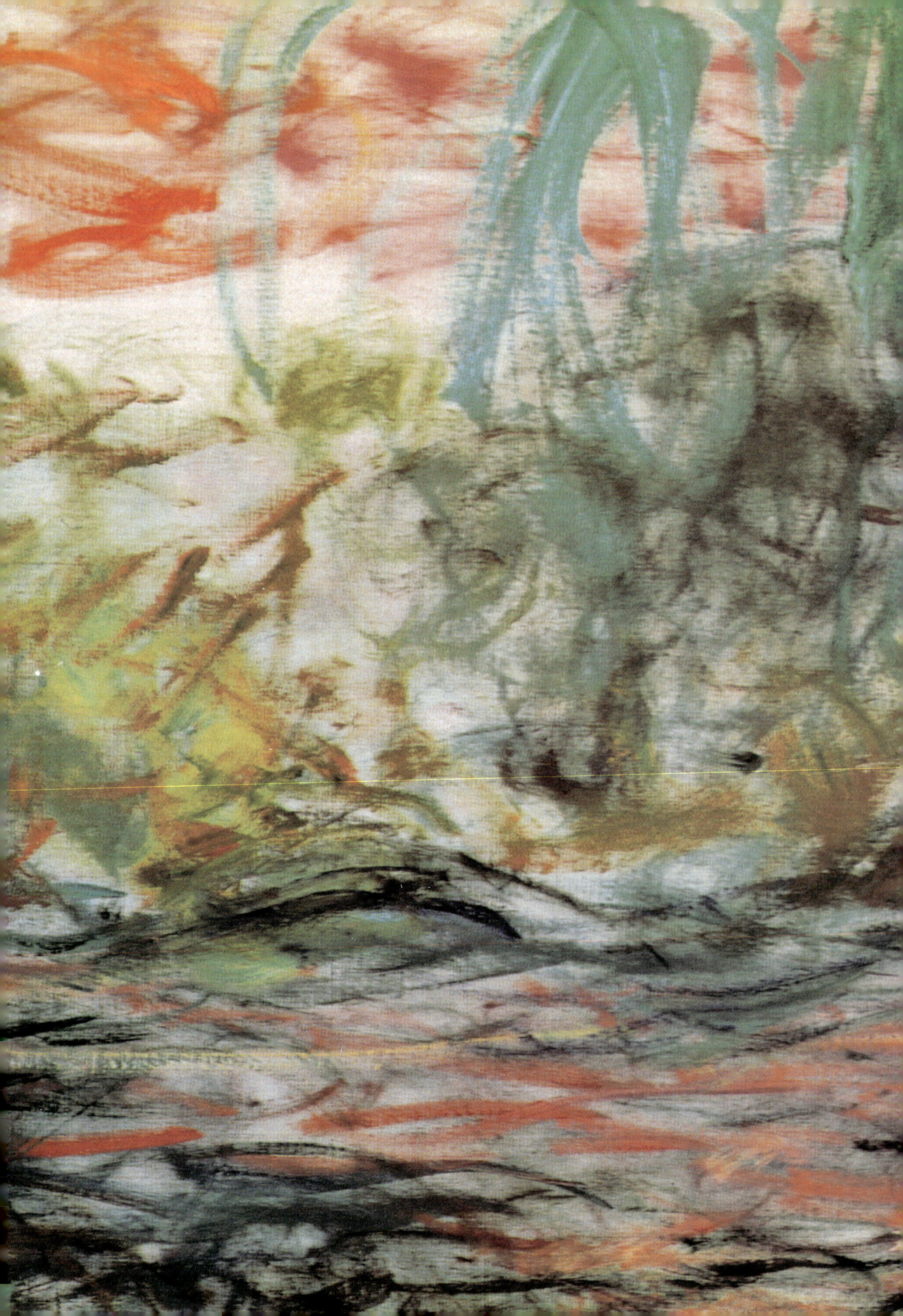

WATER FEATURES

garden ponds quarterly   water features

If you have a stream or a lot of land, you can make a circular canal with bridges, rowboats and trees...this sort of thing can double the value of your property by draining excess water and beautifying it with water plants and game fishes.

water features

RIVERS AND WATERFALLS

The soil excavated from the hole can be used to create a higher level around the back and sides of your pond. This can be turned into a rockery and/or used to create a miniature river or waterfall. There are plenty of prefabricated water courses and miniature ponds with a lip available which will create a river and waterfall. These are installed in the same way as a prefabricated pond with the lower levels positioned first. A water pump is positioned in the main pond and a hose attached to the outlet and run up to the top pond or start of the water course. Apart from the fact that it looks obviously contrived, the only problem you are likely to encounter is if you buy a pump which is not strong enough to pump the water up to the top of the water course. Most pumps give you the flow rate and the height to which the pump will raise water. It is this last figure which is important and must be substantially higher than the top of the water course.

A much better and more natural looking river and/or waterfall with bog garden area can be created using a pond liner. Often the off cut from your main pond will do the trick. For a basic one foot wide river without top pond this needs to be five feet in width and three feet longer than the water course you want to create.

First of all, dig out the water course a foot wide and about a foot deep. The slope should not be too steep and the best looking design tends to be a gently undulating one to mimic a natural river course. Now remove $1\ ^1/_2$ feet of soil along each bank. This should be dug down to a depth of ten inches by the water course and gently slope up to the surrounding soil level. Next, go over the whole water course and remove any sharp stones or other objects which might puncture the liner.

Now position the water pump in the main pond and run a hose from its outlet up

> A rocky waterfall at Longwood Gardens, Pennsylvania. Only a part of this particular waterfall (five separate levels) is shown here.

water features

to the top of the water course. This can be placed under the bog garden area where the liner and soil will hide it.

The liner can now be placed in the water course. This should overlap the edge of the main pond where it is often a good idea to make a small waterfall. This can easily be achieved using a piece of paving stone under the water course liner which protrudes over the edge of the pond. Another flat stone is then positioned on top of the liner (slate is good for this) and stones are used to disguise the edges.

If you are having a small top pond at the other end of the water course, then its liner must now be positioned with the edge overlapping the water course liner. Once again a waterfall can be created at this point.

Once your liners are in position, lay a line of stones along both edges of the water course, leaving the main water course clear, and position the end of the hose from your pump so it will direct the flow of water into the water course or top pond. Stones, turf or plants can be used to hide where it emerges from the soil. Next switch on the pump and check the water flow. It should run down the main water course and can flow up into the bog garden area a little but must not overflow the edges of your liner either in the bog garden area or where water enters your main pond. Once you are sure everything is flowing correctly and the water course holds water, you can move on to the bog garden.

First of all mix the bog garden's soil. If you have a rich very fertile soil which retains moisture well, then you will only need to mix 1 part of rotted cow or horse manure to every 4 parts of garden soil. Light loamy soils which dry out quickly and are free draining will need 2 parts manure to 3 parts soil, while heavy clay soils will only need the addition of bone meal. If your soil is almost pure clay, it is a good idea to take this opportunity of mixing it with a good garden loam to improve the texture. Generally mix an equal amount of loam into the clay. Once mixed, the garden soil can be shovelled into place behind the stones.

Now plant up the bog garden (see the separate chapter for which plants to use) and water everything in thoroughly. This is important with all plants but with bog plants it is absolutely essential. Once you have finished you can switch on the pump and stand back to admire

Photo by Michael Gilroy.

Looking down on a waterfall can be exciting! What a lovely addition to a rock water garden.

water features
Photo by Michael Gilroy.

23

A magnificent rock and water garden, including a bog garden (not shown) at the base of the waterfall.

Waterfall, bridge, water lilies and flowering border plants make this the dream water garden.
Photo by Michael Gilroy.

water features

All photographs by Michael Gilroy.

An expensive metal statue water fountain.

Pumping water to the top, then allowing it to run back into the water garden, is a delightful way to make a waterfall.

Concrete fountains are the least expensive, and they are decorative and effective.

your work. It will take a few years for everything to settle down and really start to grow but the final effect can be really stunning.

FOUNTAINS

Fountains have been an important part of ornamental ponds for thousands of years. Originally they had to have water channeled down to them from mountain springs but with the advent of electric water pumps anyone can have one in their pond. My own feeling about them is that they have little place in a natural, informal pond but are an essential part of any formal pond.

If you do decide to include a fountain in your pond, make sure it is positioned well clear of any water lilies and be careful not to have one which shoots the water too high into the air. In a strong wind it is amazing how far water can be carried and it is very easy to empty a pond in only a matter of a few hours. So keep it small and in proportion to its surroundings and check on your pond's water level every so often.

One fountain which does not look out of place in a natural informal pond is a cobble fountain. This is easily made by creating an island from stones with a hose buried in it which runs down to the outlet of a water pump. At the apex of the island, water can be allowed to bubble up out of the rocks to recreate the look of a natural spring. Bog plants can be grown in pots hidden in the stones or you can wrap a piece of turf around their roots and push this between the stones to provide a growing medium. In time a very natural looking feature will be created.

An elaborate water garden fountain.

Oriental bamboo fountain. The water is pumped to the top of the bamboo drain.

A typical water fountain from a converted drinking fountain.

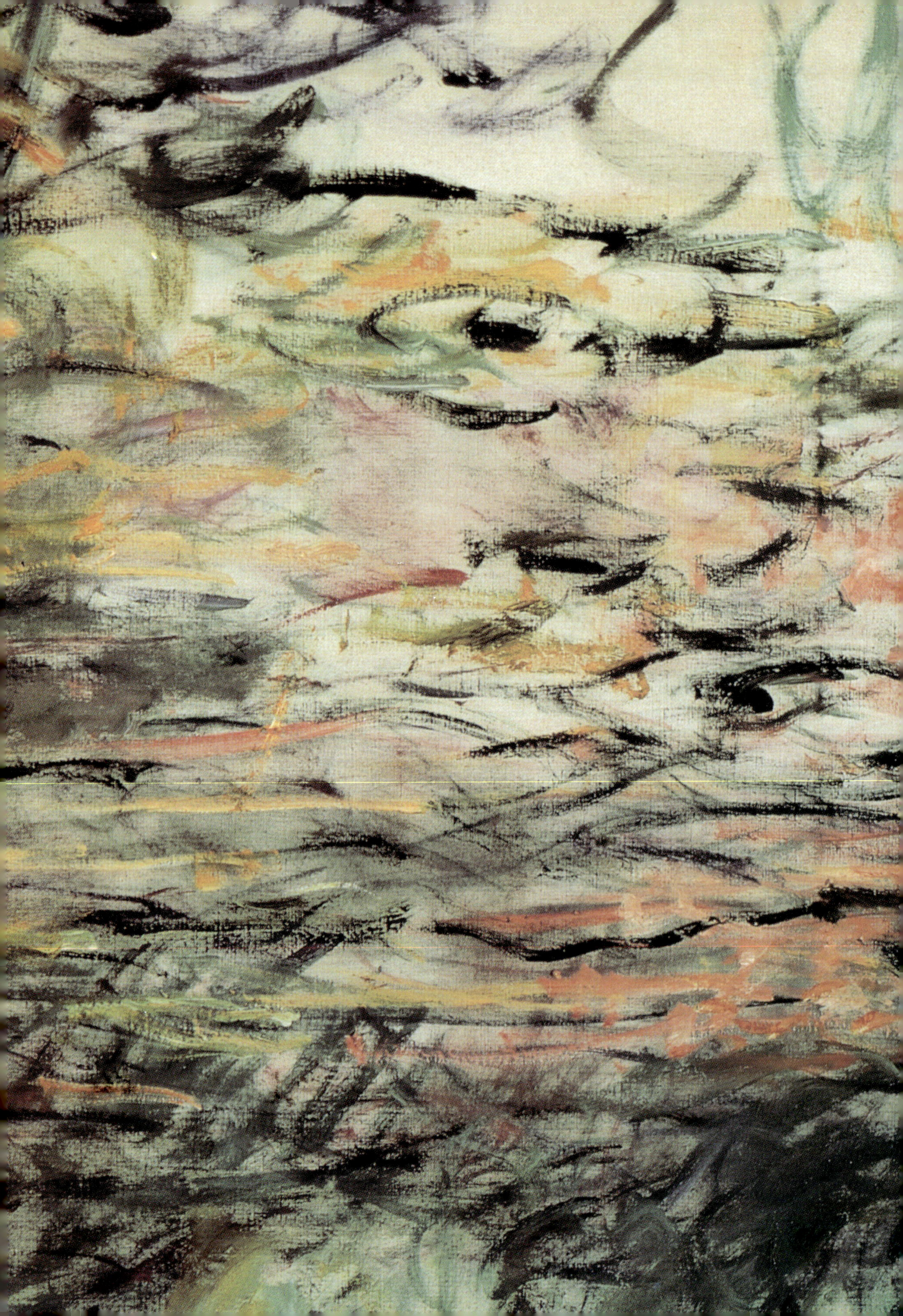

FILTRATION & POND MAINTENANCE

filtration & pond maintenance

The health of plants, fish, amphibians and other life in your pond will depend on the water they live in. If the water becomes polluted then disease and death will surely follow. In any natural pond a balance has developed between animals and plants so that the waste products produced by animals are broken down by bacteria and plants, hence keeping the water pure and healthy. For a healthy pond we must try to recreate this balance.

If enough growing aquatic plants are living in the pond, they will act as natural filters and maintain a healthy environment. The problems start when there are not enough plants or too many fish. Ammonia, nitrites and nitrates start to build up and will eventually poison the fish and other animals. So, how many are 'enough' growing plants? This is a tricky question to answer but I work on about 1/3 of the pond area having growing aquatic plants in it, excluding the lilies.

The other side of the equation is how many fish are 'too many'? Here we have to take into consideration the size and type of fish as well as number. It is advisable to allow 1 sq ft. of surface area per 1 inch of eventual fish size. So a pond 10 ft. by 6 ft. which has a surface area of 60 sq ft. can hold 60 inches of fish. Just because you are stocking your pond with small fish only 2" long, however, does not mean you can have 30 fish. You have to work on the fishes' eventual size which for Goldfish may be 6". Therefore, your pond can only hold 10 fish if you want to maintain a healthy environment.

If you are planning to have Koi in your pond then you will not be able to create the natural balance outlined above because these fish produce huge amounts of waste and like nothing better than to dig up and eat aquatic plants. You could partition off part of the pond and keep the fish away from the plants but this does not solve the basic problem of the large amount of waste produced by these beautiful fish.

The only solution is, therefore, artificial filtration. There is a bewildering array of

A three-colored Koi with a tancho head marking. The *tancho* is a Japanese stork with a red mark on the head. This is a favorite fish because its head resembles the Japanese flag.

A two-colored Koi. Koi are the best fishes for water gardens because they are large, colorful and hardy.

different types available now and more coming on the market all the time. Look for one capable of coping with the volume of water in your pond and try to find a combined unit which has a U.V. sterilizer built in. If money is at a premium, then stick with Goldfish rather than Koi and aim for a balanced environment.

One mechanical unit which may be worthwhile buying even if you don't have a filtration system is a U.V. sterilizer. This works by killing the single-celled algae which cause green water and helps prevent your pond looking like a bowl of pea soup.

filtration & pond maintenance

POND MAINTENANCE

Apart from taking out any dead leaves, fish or other animals and topping up the water when it evaporates, maintaining your pond during much of the year is easy. If the water turns whitish then there is a major problem usually involving a dead body or bodies in the pond. Check the whole pond over carefully and once the source of the problem has been removed do a large water change right away followed by another a few days later. Quick action at this time will save the lives of your fish.

Blanket weed is one problem which is almost certain to turn up. This is a filamentous algae which grows anchored to any suitable object. The pond sides and plant containers are favorite places for it to form but in bad cases this will smother growing plants as well. Removal of this pest can be easily achieved using a piece of wood with a couple of nails hammered part way into it. If this is stuck into the threads and twisted, huge chunks of algae will become tangled up with it and can be pulled out. It is a good idea to do this every few weeks.

If a filter has been installed then this must be cleaned regularly. The bulbs of U.V. sterilizers have a finite effective life and will have to be replaced every year or so. When they have reached the end of their life, algae will no longer be killed and your water will turn green again.

A proper clean-up has to be undertaken in late Fall. This means netting out all the dead leaves which have fallen in the water and cutting back the submerged oxygenating plants to a few inches of growth. All the old water lily leaves which have started to rot must be removed and a partial water change is a good idea. Any delicate plants which require winter protection should be moved under cover before the first frosts and any which are going to be left in place must be covered. It is a good idea to collect

Kits that include essential water treatment and conditioning products are available, generally at prices that are less than would have to be charged for the products if purchased separately. Some such kits also include instructional booklets and free samples of other products. Photo courtesy of Jungle Laboratories Corporation.

seeds or take cuttings or divisions from these plants so you have backup stock if a particularly harsh winter kills the parent plants.

Little can or needs to be done during winter except clean snow off the ice after it has fallen. This helps reduce the risk of aquatic plants dying due to lack of light. If this happens there is a real risk the fish may die as well. Many people worry about the formation of ice on their pond and try to find ways of keeping at least a hole open all the time. Small pond heaters can be purchased to do this job or you can melt a hole using boiling water. Covered with sacking this should stay open for a time and allow some exchange of gases. Personally, I have rarely bothered with this and, so far (fingers crossed), I have never lost fish during the winter months. Most winter fish kills I have heard about seem to stem from not cleaning up the pond properly in the autumn. Rotting organic matter produces noxious gases which will kill fish when it is trapped in the pond under the ice.

Spring is another very busy period for the water gardener because this is the time many marginals need dividing and replanting. Water Lilies will also need dividing and replanting in fresh soil. This should be done every 3 or 4 years if you want to maintain good levels of flowering. Late Spring is also a good time to buy new plants and fish for a pond. Make sure these are properly quarantined before they are introduced.

One of the most important things to do any time of the year is, once all the work has been done, stand back and take time to look at your pond and watch the fish. Take pleasure in your achievements and enjoy the beauty and tranquility of the scene. *This is what water gardening is all about.*

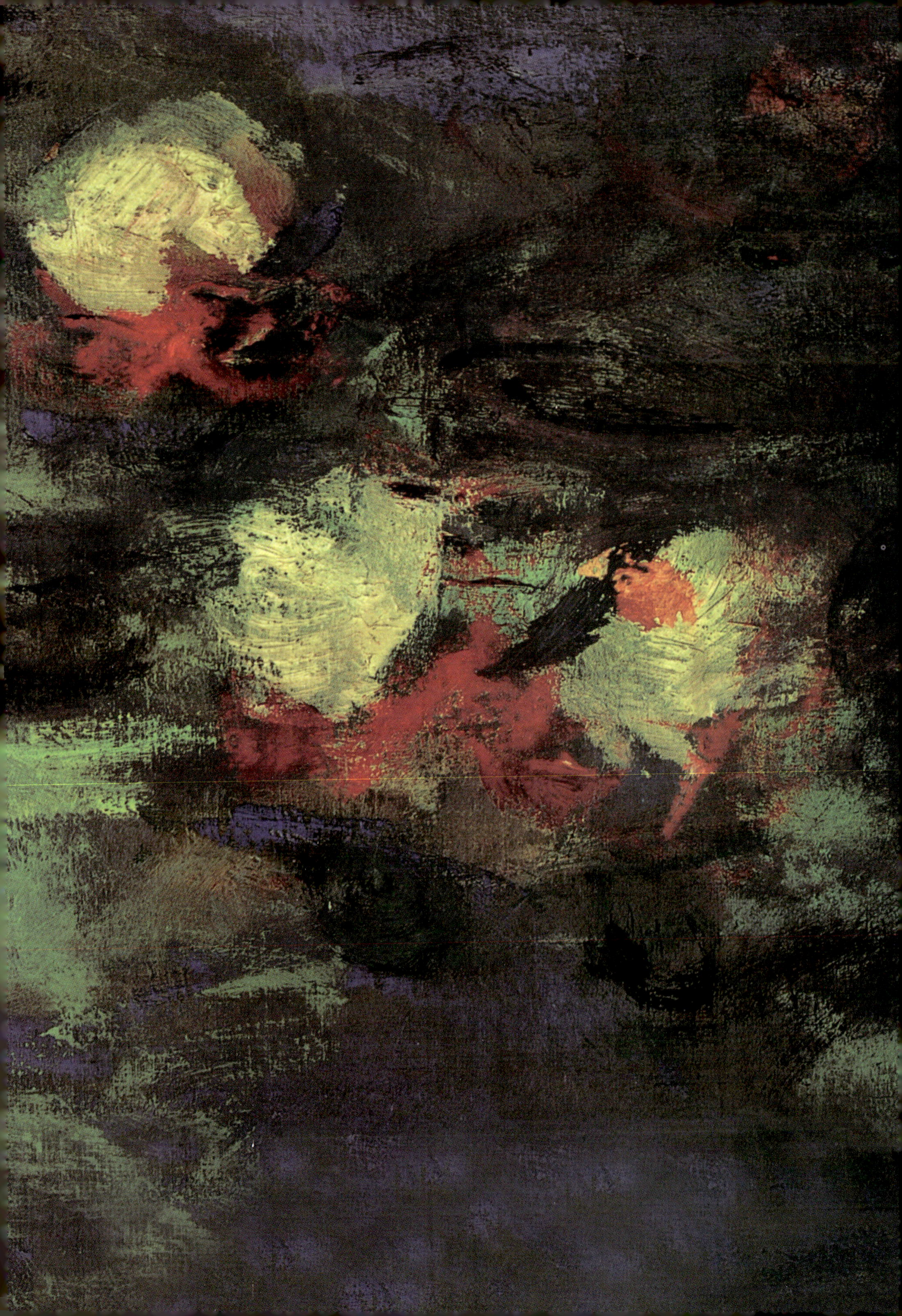

AQUATIC PLANTS

aquatic plants

Aquatic plants form an integral part of a healthy aquatic environment which can add greatly to the natural beauty of a pond and play a vital part in its well-being. For simplicity I am including floating plants as well as anchored, submerged aquatics in this section because some plants can be found floating on or near the surface for some of the year but also spend some of it submerged.

Where roots develop it is a good idea to plant these in containers or pots of soil. Use seven parts sterilized meadow loam and one part rotted cow or horse manure to fill these. Once the plant is in position, cover with a layer of gravel to keep the soil in place. Some people cover the bottom of their pond with soil and plant directly into this. The problem with this is that some plants will spread with alarming speed and smother everything, whilst others need to be divided or trimmed back every year and working thigh deep in water to do these jobs is not a pleasant experience. If the plants are in containers all you have to do is lift them out of the pond and work on them in the relative comfort of dry land.

The following is a list of the more commonly found species and varieties.

Aponogeton distachyos

The Water Hawthorn is one of the best deep water aquatics for the garden pond. It can be grown in water of up to 30 inches in depth and produces long strap-like floating leaves. During spring and fall lovely scented white flowers made up of two distinct spikes are produced in profusion. These

Aponogeton distachyos.

are held just above the water's surface and look for all the world like a group of beautiful butterflies have settled on the plant. Propagation is by seeds which the plant produces in abundance or by division in the spring.

Azolla caroliniana

This floating plant can become an absolute pest in a garden pond. In bright sunlight it will reproduce rapidly

Azolla caroliniana.

and within a very short time cover the whole surface of a pond. Once this happens the plants below will be starved of light. Water quality will suffer as a result. For this reason it must be thinned every few weeks to keep its growth under control. The pretty green fern-like leaves will develop a reddish tinge in strong light and turn bright red in autumn. When the first hard frost bites the foliage is killed off and falls to the bottom where it rots, although some plants may remain dormant over winter and recolonize the pond next year.

Ceratophyllum demersum

This is a rootless plant which tends to float beneath the water's surface. It has

Ceratophyllum demersum.

whorls of rigid dark green leaves on rather fragile stems. In good light it will grow very rapidly and send out lots of side shoots producing a large mass. It will sometimes anchor itself to the substrate with rootlike structures called *rhizoids.* Propagation is easy by taking cuttings from the main stems or from side shoots which break off the main plant. This is a valuable plant for shady ponds because it will continue to grow even in relatively poor light.

aquatic plants

Photo by Dr. Herbert R. Axelrod.

Eichhornia crassipes.

Eichhornia crassipes

This plant has caused widespread devastation in tropical areas where it grows so rampantly that it clogs up the rivers and causes the fish to die of oxygen starvation. The leaf stalk is a bloated spongy ball which is filled with air and keeps the plant afloat. During the summer months hyacinth-like flowers are produced above the foliage. This is a tropical species which will be killed by the first frost of the year. Since the rotting foliage will pollute the water it is important to remove the dead plants as soon as possible. Propagation is by runners and plants can be overwintered in an aquarium or bucket kept in good light at a minimum temperature of 65 °F.

Elodea canadensis, left, Elodea densa, right.

Drawings by Mirko Vosatka.

Eleocharis acicularis

This rather unusual plant with thread-like leaves forms dense areas of turf-like growth. Depending on the conditions, it may reach a height of 9 inches but may be limited to only 2 inches high if grown in boggy soil rather than underwater. It is a good idea to divide and replant part of the clump when it fills its container or at least every year to help stimulate new growth. Apart from this division, propagation is by runners.

Fontinalis antipyretica.

Elodea canadensis

This is one of the most useful and commonly found oxygenators. It is normally sold in bunches bound together by pieces of lead or rubber band. These should be separated and each stem planted individually. Once established, these form dense branching mats of growth which are a haven for insects, newts and small fish. Propagation is by cuttings taken from the side shoots. If not cut back and grown in a container this plant can become invasive.

Eleocharis acicularis.

Fontinalis antipyretica

This lovely dark green moss-like plant is something of a problem to grow. It requires fast-moving soft water, bright light and needs its wiry roots to be attached to stone, brickwork or other solid surface. This means it can only really be established next to the filter outlet or under the cascade created by a waterfall. Its other requirement of soft, slightly acidic water means it can only really be kept in areas where the tap water is similar to this. Should you be lucky enough to find and establish some of this plant, propagation is by layering or from side shoots.

Hottonia palustris

The Water Violet produces lovely spikes of white to pinkish flowers which reach up to 14 inches above the water's surface in the summer. Most of the leaf growth is below the surface and consists of dense whorls of heavily divided light green leaves. This plant overwinters in the form of turions resting on the substrate. Propagation is by stem cuttings taken in late spring to early summer.

aquatic plants

Hottonia palustris.

Hydrocharis morsus-ranae

This is a miniature floating water plant with small kidney shaped leaves. Above the leaves, three-petaled white flowers are produced during the summer. These have a lovely yellow center and resemble a miniature water lily. Despite this, it is actually a floating plant which sends out runners on which small plantlets develop. Although each plant is only four inches when full grown, the whole mass can be in excess of three feet across. Propagation is by removing runners with a well developed plantlet on them. This should be done no later than August which will allow the plant enough time to reach maturity before winter sets in. During Autumn resting buds are produced which drop to the bottom of the pond and overwinter there while the rest of the plant disintegrates. This plant prefers still water and is often the victim of snails which eat all parts of it.

Hydrocharis morsus-ranae as it exists in Nature in Brazil.

Lagarosiphon major

A similar plant to *Elodea canadensis*, this has longer leaves which curve strongly downwards towards the stem. It is a slower growing and less invasive species which tolerates warmer temperatures better than *E. canadensis*. Propagation is by cuttings taken from the side shoots. These should be planted in groups of three to five in a 6-inch pot and positioned in a shallow area of the pond.

Lagarosiphon major.

Lemna

Duckweeds of various types seem to pop up in every pond from time to time. The problem with this pest is it will reproduce so rapidly the whole surface becomes covered, causing light deprivation to the plants growing (now dying) beneath. For this reason you have to remove as much of it as you can as often as you can. If you have a Duckweed-free pond at the moment try to keep it that way. Wash all new plants thoroughly and keep them in a quarantine tank for a few weeks.

Lemna, Duckweed.

Myriophyllum spp.

There are several species of Parrot's Feather which are sold as oxygenators or even as marginals. In reality they are all really true aquatics which send their stems up to the surface and have the bulk of their leaves above the water line. Here flowers develop and the lovely feathery foliage can be seen to best advantage. Just how much oxygenation takes place below the water line is in doubt but it is worth

Myriophyllum, Parrot's Feather.

aquatic plants

having just for its appearance. Propagation is by cuttings both of the main stem and from side shoots.

Photo courtesy of Aqua Mart, Inc., Orlando, Florida.

Nelumbo species are lotus plants. This shows a beautiful lotus blossom.

Nelumbo spp

Lotus plants are grown for their lovely blue-green leaves which are up to two feet across and often held as much as six feet above the water. The beautiful flowers are produced throughout the summer and are held above the foliage. They can measure up to one foot across. These plants need rich soil and a container at least three feet across and a foot deep. When planting the tuber, the thick end should be 2" under the soil while the sharp growing point is held just clear of the soil. To start with, have only a few inches of water over the plant but as it grows this can be increased to two feet. Most species and hybrids are tender but it is supposed to be possible to have them overwinter in those areas where the tuber receives lots of hot summer sun to ripen it. Continental Europe and much of America fit this description but sadly the U.K. does not. Propagation is by seeds or division in the spring.

Nuphar spp.

The spatterdocks are the "Poor Man's Water Lily". They have thick oval leaves which float on the water's surface in a similar fashion to water lilies. The flowers, however, are single, much smaller in size and mostly produced in shades of yellow. So why keep these obviously inferior plants? Well they are ideal in deep water conditions (six feet is fine for some species), thrive in acid water (which most lilies hate) and will grow and even flower in a shaded position. Add to this a tolerance of flowing water (which lilies do not have) and you have some pretty compelling

Nuphar luteum.

reasons to use these plants instead of water lilies in some circumstances. They have a creeping root stock which can be four inches thick and may grow as long as six feet. Propagation is by seed or division of the root stock but side shoots of the rhizome are only rarely formed so suitable opportunities for this are rare.

Nymphaea spp.

Water lilies are not really considered an optional *extra* when it comes to a pond, but an absolute *necessity*. There are huge numbers of species and hybrids available but it is very easy to acquire a variety which is too vigorous for your pond. The vigorous types tend to be more commonly available and cheaper but they can dominate all but the largest of ponds. When you buy a lily it should have a description containing planting depth and spread. As a rough guide a small pond can accommodate lilies with a spread of up to six feet, while medium ponds can cope with up to nine feet and large ponds and lakes need vigorous lilies with a spread of ten feet and above. Along with increased spread goes increased planting depth. It is important to make sure you select a lily which can cope with the depth of water in your pond.

All varieties need an open, sunny site and still water to thrive. They should be planted in a rich soil made up of one part rotted cow or horse manure to four parts sterilized meadow loam. This should be topped off with an inch or two of coarse gravel to prevent the soil from being stirred up every time a fish grubs about the planting grate. This is especially important if you keep Koi or Tench in the pond.

Two distinct kinds of root stock are found and these must be treated differently. If you have a lily with a conical rootstock with its growing point at the apex then they need to be planted upright with the growing point above the compost. The other type of rhizome grows almost horizontally and must be planted this way with the growing tip just showing above the soil's surface.

Every three to four years it is necessary to lift and divide all lilies. This should be done in spring or early summer and becomes essential when overgrown lilies produce leaves which stand up high above the water surface. If it is a new lily then this may be

Nymphaea Shirley Bryne water lily.

the result of planting a vigorus variety in water which is too shallow but otherwise it is a sign that you need to divide your lily. To do this, lift the container out of the water and wash of all the soil from your lily roots. Now cut off any mature buds and look closely at the rhizome. You should be able to see quite a few young side shoots with leaves coming out of them. Each one of these needs cutting off with a piece of the rhizome and some roots attached to it. The old central core of rhizome is then discarded and each of the new plants potted up and placed back in the pond.

Nymphaea St. Louis Gold water lily.

Nymphaea Fabiola water lily.

Some people recommend raising the planting basket so the soil surface is only 4 to 6 inches deep until the leaves have reached the top and then lowering the basket progressively deeper until it rests on the bottom. When I first bought a lily no one told me to do this so I just dropped it in place. Since then I have always done this and all my lilies have thrived. If it is wrong then someone should tell the lilies this!

Nymphoides peltata.

Nymphoides peltata

The Water Fringe is a rapidly growing shallow water plant which can become invasive if not contained. It has two-inch floating leaves which look a lot like water lily leaves and pretty yellow flowers which are held above the water's surface. It thrives in shallow water some four to twelve inches deep. It will send out runners throughout the growing season which can be detached and established as separate plants.

Orontium aquaticum

The lance-shaped leaves of this plant will float or stand up above the water's surface depending upon the water depth it is grown in. It can be used as a marginal but does better when grown as a true aquatic in water 18 inches deep. During the summer, flower spikes are sent up above the foliage. The last few inches of these are yellow while the rest is white. Propagate by fresh seeds collected in midsummer.

Orontium aquaticum.

Pistia stratiotes

One of the better tropical floating plants which is worthwhile introducing to a pond once all danger of frost has passed. It develops a rosette of velvety leaves and a clump of finely branched roots below. It prefers still water so must be kept away from the fountain or waterfall. Propagation is by runners which are freely produced during the growing season. Remove all plants from the pond before the first frost and keep them in an aquarium kept in a warm, well lit place. If you have too many plants for the holding tank select small plants rather than the large ones to keep over winter.

aquatic plants

Potomogeton crispus.

Potamogeton crispus

This lovely plant has the appearance of seaweed with four-inch-long crinkly leaves on a main stem. Depending on lighting these can be green or flushed bronze. It prefers an open sunny site with some water movement. Propagation is usually by cuttings but during the summer seed will develop from the flowers produced on stems held above the water line. These can be collected when ripe. Ideally this plant likes to have a clay substrate in which to grow but will adapt to most soil conditions.

Pistia stratiotes.

Photo by Tomey.

Ranunculus aquatilis

A deep water aquatic plant which can grow in water up to two feet deep. This plant is useful because it produces a mass of kidney-shaped floating leaves and finely divided submerged leaves which act as oxygenators. It produces pretty little buttercup-like flowers which are white with a yellow throat. This is a very vigorous species which is best suited to large pools where it will have the room to grow. Propagation is by fresh seed or division in the Spring or Autumn.

Stratiotes aloides.

Stratiotes aloides

I have had Water Soldiers in every pond I have ever owned. This evergreen plant has stiff narrow leaves which come to a sharp point and are arranged in a rosette around a central crown. They are neither a floating plant nor a permanently submerged plant. During the summer months they rise from the bottom to rest partially above the water's surface. In hard water they tend to show above the surface more than in soft but no one has ever figured out exactly why this should be so. From early summer through to the end of August they produce a series of white flowers which are held above the water's surface. By the first frost, though, they have returned to the pond's bottom and rooted themselves in the substrate. Here they act as valuable oxygenators throughout the winter months. Propagation is by separating runners from the parent plants during the summer months.

Trapa natans

This is a difficult plant to cultivate but has rather nice floating fringed green leaves with red stalks. The leaves emerge alternately from the main stem which can grow as long as 15 feet. Principally a floating plant, the main stem

Trapa natans.

must be anchored in the substrate for it to do well. It is also fussy about water conditions and needs soft acid water to thrive. Propagation is by lateral shoots which are runner-like in appearance.

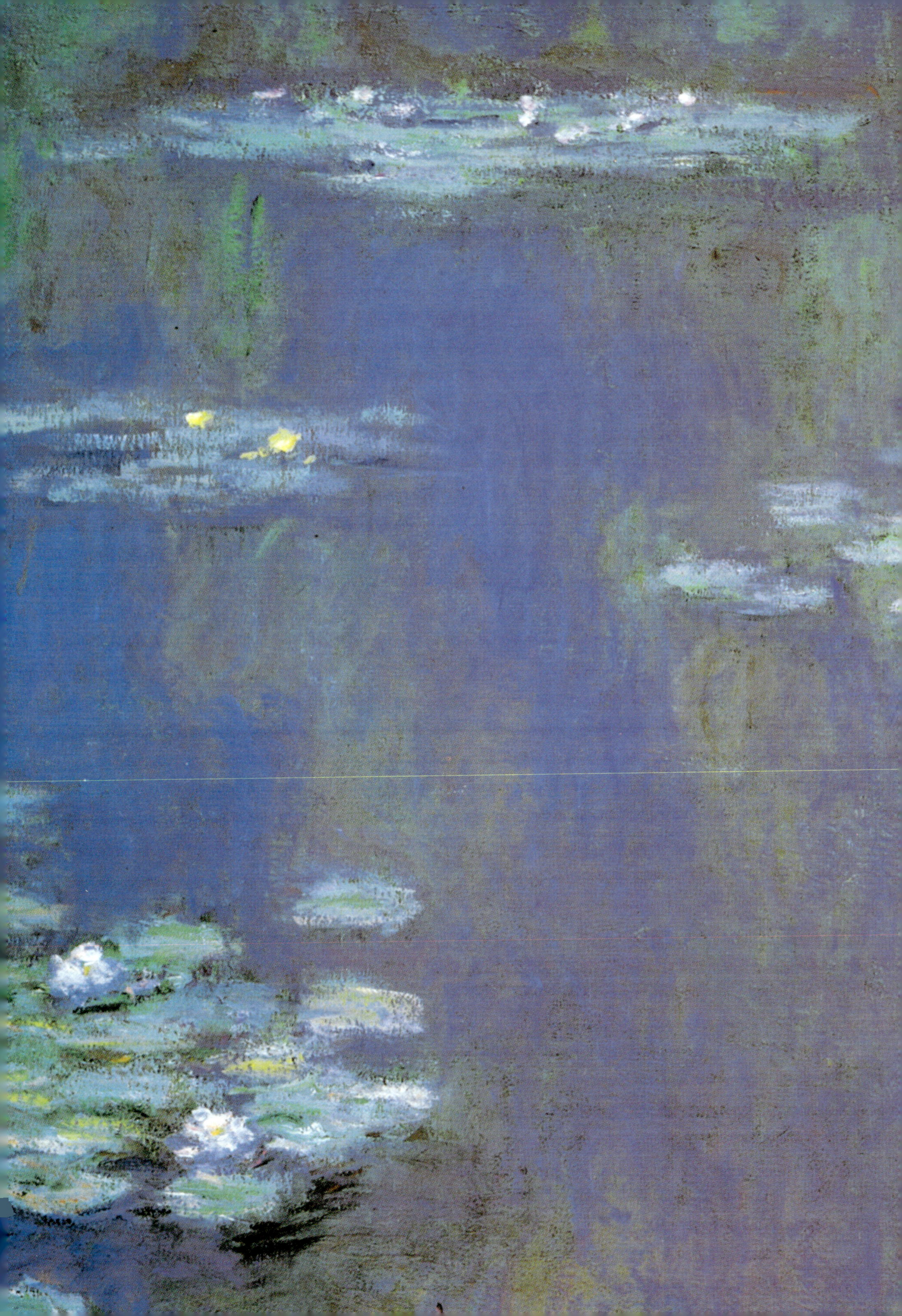

THE BOG GARDEN

the bog garden

One of the problems in trying to create a natural looking pond is how to progress from a purely aquatic habitat to dry land. In nature this transition is not normally directly from one to the other but is a slow change with an area of boggy land in between. In a garden setting this natural progression can be recreated by making an artificial bog garden either as an integral part of the pond or as a separate entity which is located next to it. Of the two, my own preference is for a separate bog garden because it is easier to maintain the environment this way and if you do put a garden fork through the liner, you will not do any harm to the main pond. I will, however, be covering both methods in this chapter.

CREATING A SEPARATE BOG GARDEN

All you need for this is a piece of two-inch-wide pipe about eighteen inches long and a spare piece of pond liner or even heavy duty polyethylene sheeting. This will need to be two feet longer and wider than the bog garden you want to create. In most cases you will also need some well rotted horse or cow manure to improve moisture retention and possibly a concentrated organic fertilizer.

First of all, dig out the bog garden to a depth of twelve inches, placing the soil nearby and any worms you find in a bucket of damp soil. Next remove any sharp stones or other objects which may puncture the liner and position this in the hole. If it is too large, cut off the excess so that the top of the liner is about an inch below the soil's surface. Now position the pipe so that its top will show above the surface and the bottom is on the base of the liner.

Next comes the most important part - mixing the bog garden's soil. If you have a rich, very fertile soil which retains moisture well, then you will only need to mix one part of manure to every four parts of garden soil. Light loamy soils which dry out quickly and are free draining will need two parts manure to three parts soil, while heavy clay soils will only need the addition of a little concentrated fertilizer such as bone meal. If your soil is almost pure clay it is a good idea to take this opportunity of mixing it with a good garden loam to improve the texture. Generally mix an equal amount of loam into the clay.

Once the soil has been mixed together this can be shoveled into the liner until it is totally covered. The bed should now be thoroughly soaked using a hose. Initially water the surface until this is wet and then place the hose into the pipe and allow it to flow for another half an hour until the soil is totally water logged. Finally, dig a hole and drop all the worms you found in the soil into it and cover them over.

CREATING A BOG GARDEN AS PART OF YOUR POND

The principles behind creating a bog garden as part of your pond are the same as

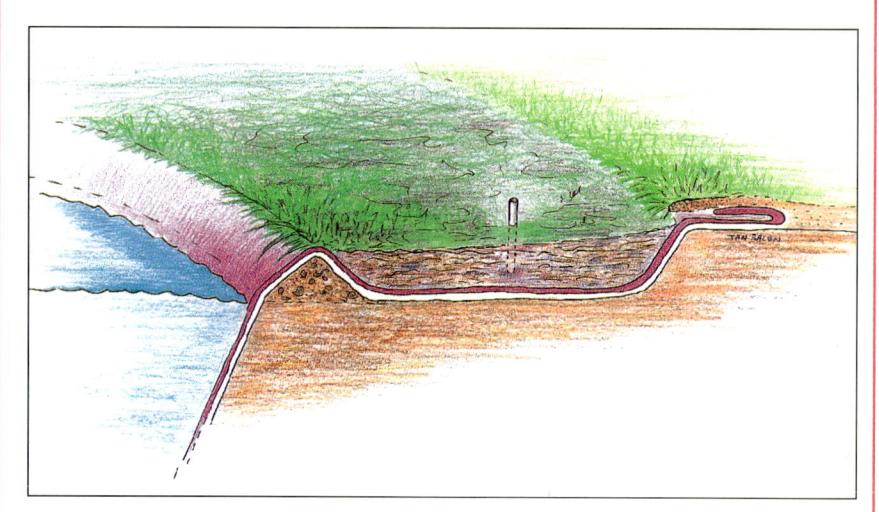

The liner under the bog garden must be large enough to contain the bog with a sufficient overlap as indicated by the heavy red line in this drawing by Jan Balon.

those already described but you use part of the pond's liner instead of a separate piece. This allows you to create a gentle slope from the water, through a boggy area, up to dry land. The problem with this is it tends to encourage evaporation from the main pond and if you accidentally put a gardening fork through the liner when digging amongst plants, the pond will lose water through it.

When you are calculating the size of your pond liner you must include the bog garden area in the calculations as well. So if the pond is 8' x 6' x 3' and the bog garden is 3' wide along one of the long

the bog garden

Photo by Michael Gilroy.

A small lovely water garden with goldfish and koi. The fish not only beautify the garden but they devour the insect larvae, thus avoiding an uncomfortable mosquito problem.

sides of the pond, the actual pond liner you need will be the same as for a pond 8' x 9' x 3'.

Apart from the larger liner size, you will also need some way of holding back the soil. This can be done by leaving a wall of earth at the front of the bog garden which is covered by the liner. This will need to be about six inches high and will form the front of the bog garden with soil sloping back from it to dry land. Alternatively, you can use rocks along the front but these need to fit closely together and be of a type safe for aquatic use. Either way the bog garden liner must rise up above the water level behind the bog garden.

The bog garden should be filled with soil as outlined above, after the pond has been filled most of the way up. Then add water until it is flooded and leave it for a few hours before planting.

PLANTING YOUR BOG GARDEN.

There is a huge range of plants available for a bog garden nowadays. Ideally it would be a good idea to buy everything you need all at once and plant the whole thing together. Unfortunately, it is often difficult to find all the plants you want at one time. Even if you did, it would leave no room for the bog garden to evolve and change as it grows. As with all plants some flourish in one situation rather than another. It is often better to try a single species or variety of a plant and see how it grows in a particular location before buying a large range of varieties and having them all fail. Once you are sure something will thrive, then you can acquire a range of them.

So, allowing for this gradual purchase of plants and testing process, it is a good idea to draw out a plan of what plants you want and where they are going to be placed. Large structural plants such as *Gunnera manicata* will need to be placed at the rear and smaller less robust plants towards the front. Those which have the same flowering season should not be placed all together but spread throughout the bed. This way something will always be of interest in a particular area rather than only one area being of interest. It is also a good idea to form clumps out of three or more of the same plants. This is particularly important with small species because an individual plant often looks lost and lonely by

the bog garden

Excavate to a depth of 8 to 16 inches depending upon the freezing conditions in the area in which you live.

THIS SERIES OF SEVEN PHOTOGRAPHS, BY ANITA NELSON, DEMONSTRATES ONE WAY TO CREATE A BOG GARDEN.

Line with scrap plastic. The bog garden does not have to be watertight.

the bog garden

> Lay in perforated pipe and attach to house rain gutter. Then cover with pea gravel.

the bog garden

Return the soil to the excavation. Mix in organic fertilizer to increase the water retention of the soil.

the bog garden

After planting you will find that the weeds take over quickly!

The weeds can be smothered using heavy mulch.

The same bog garden one year after being set up.

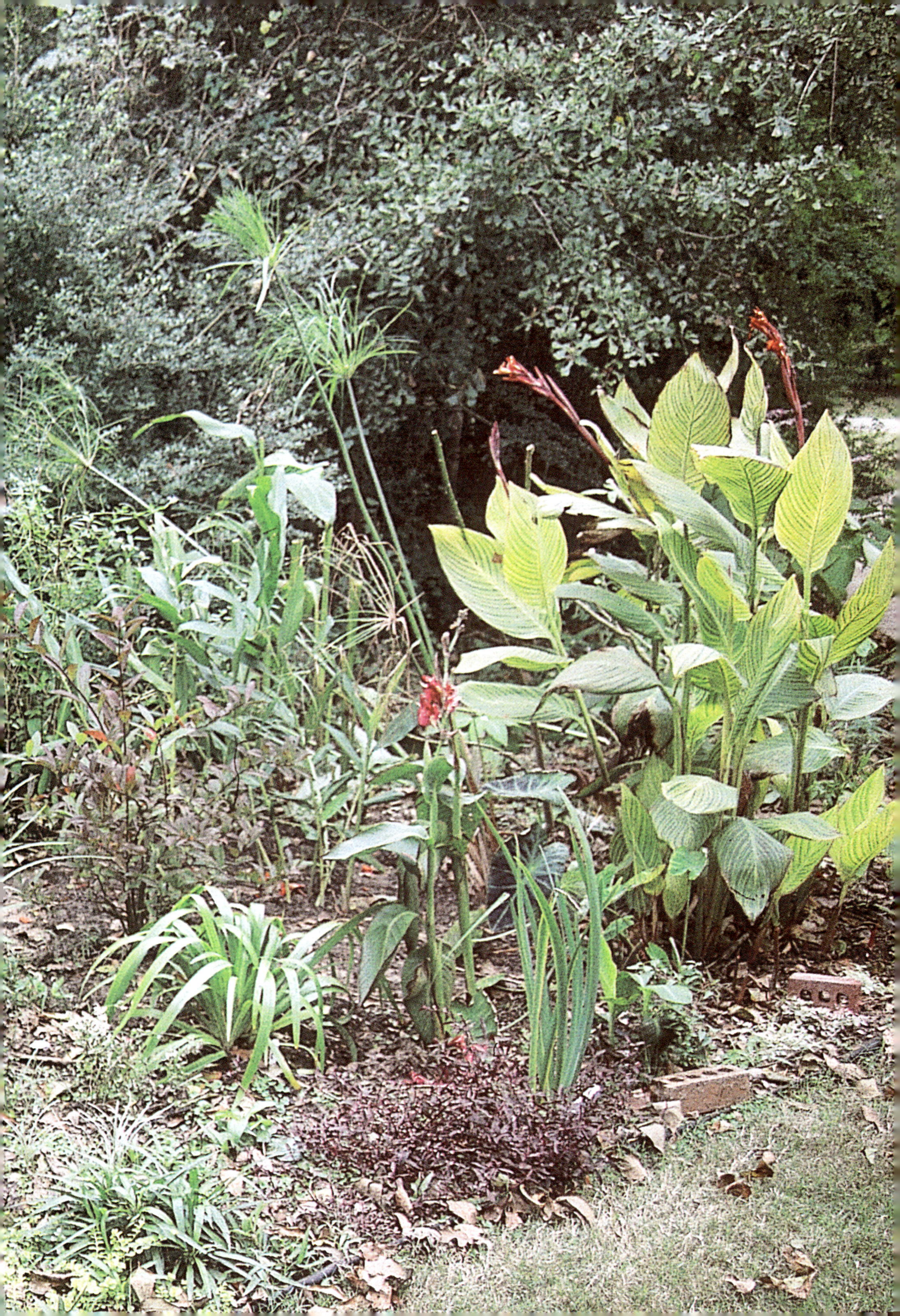

the bog garden

itself but a small group will make an impact.

Another factor to consider is that few bog plants are evergreen, so winter interest near the pond is of importance. The colored stems of some species of *Cornus* are very good for this and if you leave the leaf litter around them during winter it makes a very good home for overwintering animals.

Finally a word of warning. Some bog plants are very invasive and must have their roots restricted to prevent them overwhelming everything else in the bed. I leave these plants in their containers and either provide a shelf in the pond for them or plant them, pot and all, into the bog garden soil. These are dug up every year and re-potted. This is best done during Spring when they can also be divided or thinned out if you have too many.

MAINTAINING YOUR BOG GARDEN

Apart from regular weeding and copious amounts of water during dry spells, your bog garden will need little more than the occasional feed with a slow release fertilizer. This should be of organic origin, like bone meal, and only be used sparingly.

One good idea which is being used more and more by gardeners is mulching. This has a three-fold advantage in that it stops weed seeds from germinating, helps insulate the soil, and keeps moisture in it. There are many different kinds of mulch available but in this situation coarse bark is one of the best. Various chippings and grit can be used but these tend to look very artificial. Garden compost and peat look natural but tend to break down into the soil very quickly and provide a seed bed for any weed seed which falls on it.

When applying a mulch don't just scatter a thin layer on the soil's surface but cover it to a depth of four inches. This can be done for just a few feet around each plant (leaving the stems and growing tip clear) or the whole bed can be covered. Personally I prefer covering the whole bed because this looks more natural. Do not apply a mulch when the soil is frozen because the insulating effect will keep it cold for longer. Make sure all perennial weeds have been totally eradicated from the area.

Photo by Michael Gilroy.

Your pet shop or garden supply center should have a suitable display and variety of plants suitable for the bog garden.

SUITABLE BOG PLANTS

suitable bog plants

The following is a list of suitable plants for the bog garden. These range from some species which prefer their crowns kept just below the water's surface through to plants which only need moist conditions. Much of the literature published on ponds will give you specific planting depths for each species. I have found plants are much more accommodating than these authors make you think. Nearly all will adapt to the bog garden conditions outlined here.

Acorus

This is a genus ranging from marginal to fully aquatic plants which are hardy except in extreme conditions and are grown for their semi-evergreen leaves. Some species have scented foliage and all need a sunny open site to be at their best. In the autumn trim any leaves which die back but otherwise leave the plants undisturbed until they become congested. This may take three or four years at which time they will have to be lifted and divided. This should be done in the Spring. The best variety to buy is *Acorus calamus* 'Variegatus' which has green and white striped leaves some 30" long.

Alisma

This is a genus ranging from marginal to aquatic plants grown for their foliage and flowers. However, they have a habit of running wild if care is not taken to control them. Mine (*Alisma plantago*) just 'turned up' all of their own accord and I have been waging a losing battle against them ever since. One method of control is to remove the flower heads before the seeds are ripe but for some reason mine always seem to beat me to the draw and scatter their offspring everywhere. Common varieties include *Alisma plantago* which grows to 24" tall and has tiny pink flowers and *Alisma parviflora* which only grows to 15" tall and has tiny white flowers.

Butomus

This is a monotypic genus that contains a lovely flowering rush-like plant, *Butomus umbellatus*. It prefers an open sunny site and while it will grow in wet soil, it really likes to have its crown below the water's surface. Reaching a height of about three feet, it produces tall stems with clusters of pink red-centered flowers. Remove the leaves when they die back during the Fall and divide clumps in the Spring. Otherwise, propagation is by seeds sown in the Spring or late Summer.

Butomus umbellatus.

Photo by Bildarchiv Sammer.

suitable bog plants

Calla

A monotypic genus containing *Calla palustris*, the Bog Arum. This is a deciduous to semi-evergreen hardy marginal plant which is grown for its lovely white spring flowers which are followed by orange to red fruits. It has a spreading habit and reaches a maximum of ten inches in height. It likes a sunny position and can be propagated by division during Spring or from seeds in late Summer.

Calla palustris.

Caltha

This is a genus of about 20 species of deciduous bog plants which also contains a few species which are suitable for a rock garden. All are grown for their beautiful flowers during Spring and are generally hardy. The best species to look for include *Caltha palustris* which has lovely bright golden yellow flowers in early Spring and reaches a height of twenty four inches. Its double form *Caltha palustris* 'Flore pleno' has fully double flowers but tends to be smaller, only reaching ten inches tall. A white form, *Caltha palustris* 'Alba,' is also known. This has a second flowering period during the autumn but does not flower as freely as the other varieties of this species. The largest garden plant in this genus is *Caltha polypetala* which grows up to three feet tall and has single yellow flowers. Best suited to a large bog garden, it is very useful for filling big areas quickly.

Propagation of all species is by root division after the flowers have faded in early Summer or by seeds (not the 'Flore pleno' variety) collected during the Summer and sown directly into a water-logged seed compost. The seedlings can be transplanted to their permanent positions in the fall. After flowering, the flower stems of *Caltha polypetala* often produce roots at the nodes and can be pegged to the soil and allowed to fully root. These plantlets can be separated from the main plant in the fall.

Caltha palustris.

Cyperus

The sedges are a huge group of moisture-loving plants which include such luminaries as the papyrus. There are a number of useful hardy species out of more than 550 in the genus. Care has to be taken with most sedges because they can be extremely invasive with adventurous roots traveling every which way and seedlings popping up all over the place. Dead head all species before the seeds are ripe and only grow them with their roots confined in a container.

suitable bog plants

Cyperus. There are more than 550 species in this genus. This is *Cyperus helferi.*

Good species to look out for include *Cyperus longus* which can achieve a height of four feet and an infinite spread if given the chance. The dark evergreen leaves are rough edged and strongly ribbed. In mid to late Summer attractive umbels of red-brown plumes are produced. *Cyperus vegetus* is a smaller plant growing to only two feet in height and is less invasive. During Summer the stems carry green plumes which turn to brown as the season progresses.

Propagation is by division in April and May or by seeds collected when ripe and sown into wet compost from late March to early May. The seedlings should be large enough to plant into their permanent positions in early Fall.

Eriophorum

Cotton Grass, *Eriophorum angustifolium*, is one of the better grass-like plants for the bog garden. It produces tassels of cottonwool-like flowers above the foliage from June to August. It is hardy and grows to about one foot in height. Propagation is by division in Spring. While not so invasive as some, it is still a good idea to keep this plant in a container.

Glyceria

This is a genus of evergreen to herbaceous plants which are commonly called *grasses*. More often than not they are weeds rather than ornamental plants. They must always be kept under firm control by keeping them in a container. Rigorously dead head them before seeds can be set. One species is worth keeping in a bog garden and that is *Glyceria maxima* 'Variegate'. This has green, white and cream striped leaves which have a hint of pink in them during the spring. It grows up to three feet tall and is all too easy to propagate by division in Spring. This plant will choke any others planted near it, so it must be container grown.

Cyperus longus.

Gunnera

This genus of perennial plants is mainly grown for its spectacular foliage. Unfortunately they are not totally winter hardy and must have their crowns protected in winter. The most common species kept is *Gunnera manicata* which develops palm-like leaves fully five feet across and has a green flower spike in early Summer. This species is best suited to bog gardens associated with a large pond or lake. Propagation is by seeds in Autumn or Spring.

Gunnera manicata.

Houttuynia

This monotypic genus contains a lovely species with three distinct varieties. *Houttuynia cordata* has red stems and blue-green heart shaped leaves. It can reach two feet tall and is a very vigorous grower. In mid to late Summer small insignificant flowers are produced but these are surrounded by four larger white bracts which make a reasonable show. A double variety 'Flore pleno'

suitable bog plants

has been produced which has many more bracts but is less vigorous. Best of all is the variety 'Chameleon' which is also referred to as 'Variegate'. The leaves are variegated green, cream and vivid crimson. The cream and crimson cover larger areas of leaves which have grown in full sun, although it will also grow well in dappled shade.

In ideal conditions of moist to wet soil, all varieties of this plant can become invasive, spreading far and wide by rhizomes. Despite this it is worth planting in open soil rather than containers simply because it is such a good ground cover plant. Propagation is by division in Spring or Autumn with the divisions being grown on in a pot for a few months until they are established or they can be planted directly into their new position. Look for this species in the normal perennial section of your garden center as well as amongst the marginal plants.

Juncus

The Bog Rushes are a genus of some 300 species of plants which live in aquatic and bog habitats. Only a few species have found their way into cultivation so far and of these the best and most unusual is *effusus* 'Spiralis' . This fascinating plant has corkscrew shaped leaves. These can be as long as eighteen inches but because of the sprawling growth habit, the plant rarely becomes taller than eight inches. Any straight leaves which appear must be removed at once and although the plant will tolerate partial shade it does best in full sun. Propagation is by division in April or May.

Iris

The Irises are such a wonderful group of garden plants that it is not surprising so many different varieties have been developed. Some species and varieties need well drained soil while others thrive in the bog garden. The genus contains about 300 species and there are hundreds of hybrids and varieties available.

Photo by MP&C. Piednoir.

Iris laevigata.

suitable bog plants

Yellow flag iris, probably a hybrid.

Good bog garden varieties include *Iris laevigata* which has lavender blue flowers but varieties of this species come in many different colors. *Iris laevigata variegata* has the same lovely lavender blue flowers of the species but the fans of leaves are variegated green and cream. All of these tend to flower around early June and like to have their crowns covered by water.

For later flowering *Iris kaempferi* and its varieties will extend the flowering period into July. These come in single or double flowered forms with the most extravagant blooms being a double peony shape. This iris prefers moist to wet conditions but with its crown above water level. A lime hater, this species must be grown in acid soil.

For taller early flowering yellow irises select one of the *Iris pseudacorus* varieties. These grow to three feet or more in height and like to have their crowns covered in six inches of water. A variegated form is known but this tends to grow only $2^1/_2$ feet tall.

In the U.S.A., you may also come across *Iris veriscolor*. This is similar to *Iris laevigata* but with smaller flowers. It prefers water up to three inches deep and comes in blue through to wine-red color varieties. Flowers are produced from late May to early June.

Lobelia

The *Lobelia* genus contains over 200 species of plants many of which make excellent garden plants. It is almost inconceivable that a hanging basket would be without a spray of *Lobelia erinus* in it somewhere.

Although you rarely see them, there are a number of species which are suitable for the bog garden. Best of all and most commonly available is *Lobelia cardinalis*. This lovely plant grows to a height of three or even four feet and has pretty leaves and scarlet flowers.

It is not reliably hardy even in the U.K. and some seeds should be collected at the end of the season to provide back-up stock for next year if you lose those in the garden. Garden plants should have their crowns protected by leaves, straw or bracken placed over them or they should be lifted in late Fall and given some Winter protection in a cold frame. Those plants, however, which are growing in six inches of water will probably survive without this protection.

Lobelia cardinalis.

suitable bog plants

Flowering time is from July through to the end of August and seeds sown in late March will produce plants which flower in late August through to the first frosts. Apart from seeds you can propagate this species by division of the root stock in March.

Lysichiton

This genus contains two species of wonderfully exotic looking, hardy, herbaceous plants well worth adding to any bog garden. They require deep (at least eighteen inches) acid, boggy soil and do best in full sun but can tolerate partial shade. Between March and early May beautiful arum-like flowers are produced with stunning spathes. These are followed by the foliage which tends to grow very large. The larger species is *Lysichiton americanus* which reaches four feet tall and has yellow spathes up to eighteen inches high. *Lysichiton camtschatcense* only grows to three feet tall and has smaller spathes.

Propagation of both species is by seeds collected when they are ripe in late July or August. These should be directly planted into wet compost. Prick out into three-inch pots when they are large enough to handle. These must be kept wet by standing them in a tray of water. Pot on as required and plant into their permanent positions when two or three years old. Take great care not to damage the roots because this will kill the plants.

Mentha

The genus *Mentha* contains some 25 species of hardy to half-hardy plants which include the culinary herb Mint. *M. aquatica* is often found for sale as a bog plant and grows up to three feet in height. It develops spires of lilac-colored flowers in Mid-summer and these, as well as the leaves, have the distinctive pungent smell of mint. In common with all mints it is an invasive plant which can become a problem if growth is unchecked. Dead head once the flowers have faded and restrict the roots in a container. Propagation is by division of the root stock in Spring and early Summer.

Menyanthes

This is a genus of hardy perennial plants which prefer an open sunny site. Only one species is commonly found in the trade, *Menyanthes trifoliata* - the Bog Bean. This grows to about 9 inches tall and produces short spikes of white flowers during May and June. It prefers boggy soil or shallow water to a depth of 3" and can be propagated by stem cuttings taken in the spring or by division of the clumps also at this time.

Mimulus

This is a genus of about 100 species of hardy to tender annual and herbaceous perennials. They are often grown as normal garden plants but actually make very good additions to the bog garden. They should be planted in the Spring and will tolerate light shade but prefer a sunny location.

Good varieties include *M. luteus* which grows to two feet tall but can also form a dense mat only four inches high. It has lovely yellow blooms marked with reddish brown spots. These are produced from May through to early September. Another worthwhile species to look for is *M. ringens*. This grows somewhat larger reaching about $2\,^1/_2$ feet tall and has smaller lavender blue flowers which are produced from August to September.

As virtually all members of this genus are short lived, it is best to collect ripe seed from them and sow this the next Spring. Alternatively, you can divide the adult plants during Spring or take cuttings in April. In cold areas some protection will be needed to keep most of these species through the Winter.

Myosotis

This is a genus of 50 species of annual and perennial plants containing one of my favorites, the humble Forget-me-not. Even the species which are considered perennial tend to be short lived but fortunately produce ample seed which spreads itself all around and keeps the species going.

For the bog garden *Myosotis palustris* and its varieties are one of the very best blue-flowered plants you can have. It grows in a very straggly way but sends up stems of flowers above the foliage from April to July. It reaches a height of nine inches and can spread a foot each way. It is best planted in late Spring or early Fall and can be propagated by seed sown into waterlogged seed compost during April or May. Alternatively take basal cuttings in March or after the flowering period and insert these into waterlogged compost made of one part loam, one part peat and one part sand.

suitable bog plants

Pontederia cordata.

Peltandra

This genus contains a couple of worthwhile species for the bog garden. Most notable is *P. sagittifolia* which has arrow shaped leaves distinctly marked with veins and produces arum-like white flowers during early summer. These are followed by distinctive red berries. It will do well in a bog garden or can be grown submerged in up to six inches of water. Most of the other species in the genus have greenish flowers and berries, so are less desirable.

Pontederia

A genus of four species of perennial marginal plants of which only one is fully hardy. *P. cordata* grows to just over two feet high and produces small spikes of bluish-purple flowers from August to September. Although a bog plant, it must have very wet soil to do well and ideally the crowns should be covered by at least two inches of water. This is a strong growing species which does best in full sun.

Propagation is by division of the root stock in late Spring. To do this, lift the plants and cut off the side branches with a sharp blade. Replant the pieces two inches deep and keep covered with two inches of water until well established.

Ranunculus

A genus of over 400 species which include some lovely garden varieties and some utter pests. The same is true for the bog garden varieties with both commonly found species being invasive and best controlled by growing in a container.

R. aquatilis is a native species in the U.K. and can find its own way into a garden pond without too much trouble. It grows to two feet tall and produces white flowers from April to July. These should be dead headed as soon as they fade. *R. lingua* and its larger variety 'Grandiflora' can reach up to four feet tall and is even more invasive. It produces sprays of bright yellow flowers from June through August. It is important to dead head them before the seed can ripen. Despite being invasive, they are well worth including in a bog garden or marginal container, where rapid growth and a quick show of flowers is needed.

Propagation is by division in Spring or Autumn or by cuttings taken once the flowering period is over. Usually stopping the spread of these plants is more of a problem than trying to produce more!

Sagittaria

There are about 20 species in this genus most of which are tender aquatic species but

suitable bog plants

Sagittaria subulata

Sagittaria graminea var. *graminea*

Sagittaria graminea var. *platyphylla*

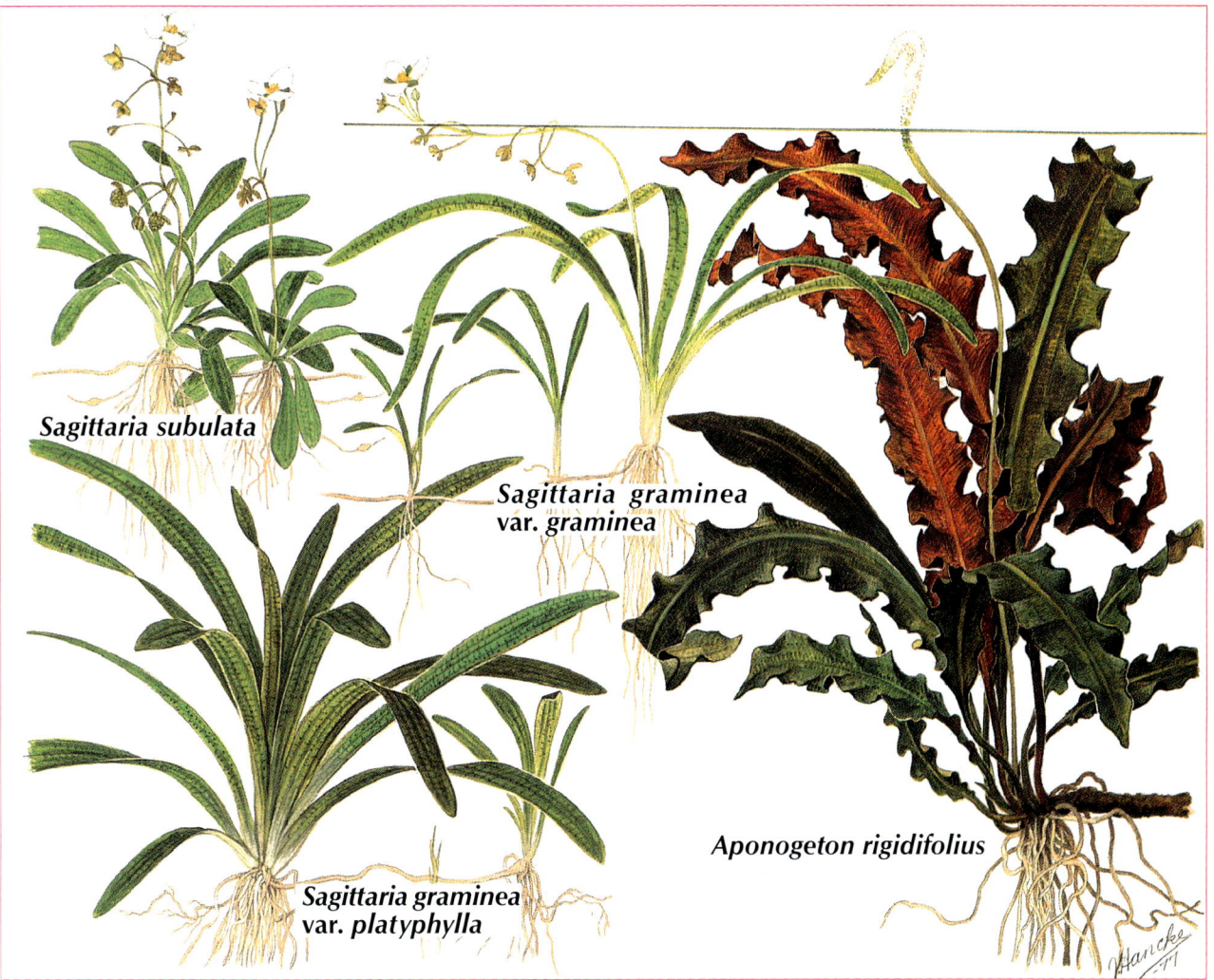

Aponogeton rigidifolius

two are hardy marginal plants which can be rather invasive if not kept under control. *S. latifolia* has two feet tall arrow shaped leaves and white flowers with yellow or green centers which are produced in July. *S. sagittaria* grows a little larger and has white flowers with a brown center. These are produced from July to August. The subspecies *S. s. leucopetala* is usually sold as *S. japonica* and produces a whorled raceme of white flowers with a yellow center. A double form of this is also known and is sold as 'Flore Pleno'.

Saururus

This is a genus of hardy perennial marginal plants of which only one is commonly available. *S. cernuus* is called the Lizard's Tail because it produces curving spikes of white flowers above the foliage. These are scented and look a lot like little curved tails. It grows to about a foot high and prefers full sun, although it can tolerate partial shade. To maintain its vigor, it should be divided every few years in the Spring.

Scirpus

This was a genus of over 300 species of plant including the Bulrush. It has since been subdivided into a number of genera but most garden centers still sell them under their old genus name of *Scirpus*. I am listing them all under this heading.

Despite the large number of species in this group very few are suitable for garden cultivation. Most are unattractive invasive weeds which grow too large for the average garden pond or bog garden. One of the few worthwhile varieties is *Schoenoplectus tabernaemontani* 'Albescens' (normally sold as *Scirpus albescens*) which grows up to six feet tall and has green and cream vertically colored stems. The best variety,

suitable bog plants

Scirpus tabernaemontani.

however, is *Schoenoplectus tabernaemontani* 'Zebrinus' (normally sold as *Scirpus zebrinus* or *Juncus zebrinus*). This only reaches three feet tall and has bands of green and white which give the *Schoenoplectus tabernaemontani* stems the appearance of porcupine quills. It is a little tender and needs Winter protection in many areas. If grown underwater, it will usually survive the Winter.

Propagation is by division of the rhizomes in April. These should be lifted and the soil washed off before cutting into segments with a sharp knife or scissors. For 'Albescens' use six inch lengths and for 'Zebrinus' use three inch lengths. Each of these must have a bud or young stem already developing.

Typha

This is a genus of about 20 hardy perennial species which are often confused with Bulrushes. All members of this genus are highly invasive and must be grown in a container if they are to be kept under control. Most species grow large and are too big for normal garden ponds; however, *T. minima* only reaches 2 $^1/_2$ feet tall and forms short plump flower heads in June and July. It is a little tender in cold areas and will only survive if the crowns are growing under water or protected by bracken or other insulating material.

Veronica

This is a large genus of over 300 species. They are mostly half hardy and hardy herbaceous perennial plants often grown for their blue flowers. Few like boggy conditions but *V. beccabunga* does well in them and is a useful plant for the pool edge. It only reaches four inches in height but can spread indefinitely. White centered blue flowers are produced from late Spring to early Summer. Propagation can be by two-inch cuttings taken in the Summer, ripe seeds sown during Spring or by division in April.

Typha latifolia grows slightly taller than *T. minima*.

Zantedeschia aethiopica.

Zantedeschia

This genus of about eight species contains a lovely half hardy marginal plant which deserves the fuss and bother of giving it winter protection. The Arum Lily reaches three feet tall and develops lovely white spathes up to nine inches long with a yellow central spadix. These appear from March to June and give the plant a very exotic look. If it is grown as a water plant with a foot of water above the plant, it may be hardy in much of the U.K. Otherwise cover the plants with bracken or straw to protect them from frosts. Better still, move them into a cold greenhouse for the winter.

Propagation is by dividing the rhizomes in October or November. The divisions should be grown on in a frost-free place during Winter and planted out when all danger of frost has passed next Spring.

A ROCKERY BY YOUR POND

a rockery by your pond

How you develop the area around your pond will greatly affect the pond's final appearance. One of the most popular features pond owners create is a rockery. This helps frame the pond and makes use of the huge quantity of soil dug out when the pond was constructed. The only problem with this type of feature is that many people think you can make a successful rockery just by piling up the soil and throwing a few stones into it. Simple as this may be, it will not produce a suitable environment for many rockery plants and the whole thing often ends up looking a complete mess. With a little thought and hard work, however, it is possible to create a wonderful rock garden which will be a thing of beauty in its own right and enhance the pond a hundredfold.

The position of your rockery is, to a certain extent, dictated by where your pond has been located. Fortunately, the needs of both pond and rockery are roughly similar; both want an open sunny site with the minimum shading from surrounding trees, hedges and buildings. You also want to avoid frost pockets and sites which are exposed to cold, drying winds. This may be impossible with some gardens, in which case you are going to have to grow tough hardy plants over much of the rockery and try to use the most sheltered positions for the more delicate species.

The stone used in your rockery is of great importance. There are many different types available from garden centers but it is often better to try to use stone from your own area. This is because it will blend in better with the surroundings than stones brought in from other places. Never mix lots of different types of stone together; this always looks contrived and artificial. It is often a good idea to visit a local quarry and select the pieces you want yourself. This usually works out cheaper and you can make sure there are lots of different sized and interesting shaped pieces. Once you have picked out the stones, have them delivered to your home and try to get them dropped off as close to the proposed rockery as possible.

Photo by Michael Gilroy.

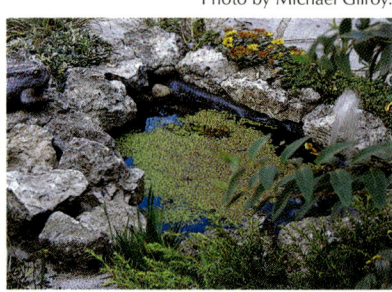

The ideal small water garden decorated with rockery.

It is very important not to use water-washed limestones in your rockery. These have been a favorite of gardeners for many years and have also been used for centuries in dry stone walls. The result is many natural habitats have been destroyed by the removal of limestone so, for conservation reasons, steer clear of these stones.

When building a rockery, the most important part of the job is to provide proper drainage. Good drainage is achieved by having a six inch deep layer of coarse rubble under the rockery. This is then covered by turfs laid upside down or a polypropylene sheet which has had holes punched over its surface. This layer allows water to pass through while keeping soil from clogging the rubble.

Once you have your base prepared, you need to sort out the soil for your rockery. Hopefully, you will be able to use the soil you dug out for the pond, but if this is heavy clay then you will have to buy good topsoil from elsewhere or bring some in from another part of the garden. To one part of garden soil mix one part peat substitute and one fine gravel or coarse grit. Once your soil has been modified and stones have been delivered you can start construction. Make sure you wear gloves and heavy boots for this job and if you are in poor health draft in some unsuspecting family member, friend (soon to become ex-friend) or pay for a workman to help you.

First of all, select some of the largest stones as your 'keystones'. These will form focal points around which various areas are developed and should be positioned first. Try to think carefully about how it will look before moving any stone; this will save a lot of unnecessary labor. Remember that any stones showing layers should be positioned in such a way that the layers are running horizontally. In most natural situations rocks tend to lie in this way so it helps add to the natural look of the finished rockery.

When the keystones are in position you can add others to build up the appearance of your first layer. Then fill in with soil and start on the next layer. Once again select some of the larger stones first and

a rockery by your pond

fill in with the smaller ones. Next fill in with soil and start on the next layer progressively using smaller stones and reducing the area covered. For stability each stone should be tilted backwards and buried in soil for about a third of its depth.

Try to leave channels between some of the stones in which plants can be grown and use enough stones to make the outcrops look realistic while leaving plenty of room for plants. It is a difficult balance to get right and one which you can only judge for yourself. Make sure all the stones are firmly bedded in position (standing on them will help do this) so that the whole construction will not move at the first downpour.

It is worthwhile positioning some of the plants as you construct your rockery. The main ones to have in place are those which are going to grow in horizontal gaps between two large stones. Once the lower stone has been firmed into position, the plants can be placed with their roots against the rock face and their crowns pointing outwards. Next using two or three pieces of wood to protect the plants lay the upper stone on top and fill in around the plants with compost. The pieces of wood can then be removed and soil or compost packed into the holes. Finally, firm the stone into position.

Alpine plants normally live in a mixture of gravel, rock debris and humus-rich detritus. This mixture drains very quickly but also retains some moisture and it is this combination of conditions that you need to recreate in the compost in which your alpines are actually grown. You will also need to take into consideration the pH of soil each alpine species requires. Some like acidic soil while others thrive in alkaline to neutral soil. To recreate these conditions, each plant is grown in a pocket of specially prepared compost.

Most alpines will thrive in a compost made from one part garden soil, one part peat substitute and one part coarse grit. This should be mixed well in a bucket before using. Those plants which come from high altitudes or

Photo by Michael Gilroy.

Can you imagine anything more peaceful and enjoyable than this rockery work of art?

require particularly good drainage will need a compost made from four parts gravel, one part peat substitute and one part garden soil. Those which need acidic conditions should be grown in a compost made from four parts peat, one part garden soil and one part coarse sand. This last group must be planted in as much of this compost as possible if your soil is naturally alkaline. It is a good idea to replace the compost every three years or at least top dress with peat every Spring.

Rock garden plants are normally sold as potted plants, so they can be purchased at any time of the year. They are, however, best planted when the weather is neither too hot nor too cold and the ground is not excessively wet or dry. Personally I try to plant mine in early spring before the plants have started into full growth.

As with all plants, water thoroughly before you plant them and then roughly place them in their proposed positions. Once you are happy with the proposed layout you can start planting them in their permanent positions. Start at the top of the rockery and work your way down. This way you are not stepping over plants which have already been bedded.

When planting, dig out a large hole and partially refill with the correct compost. Tap the pot, slide out the plant and loosen the root ball. Be careful not to damage any roots when doing this, although if they have grown through the holes in the pot's bottom, you may have to cut some of them off to release the plant. Next position the plant in the hole and fill in with more compost. Once firmed, the crown of the plant should be level with the soil unless you are planning to use a top dressing of gravel or chippings, in which case you will have to leave the plant slightly proud of the soil's surface.

When you have worked your way over the whole rockery, you should water all the plants in. If you are going

a rockery by your pond

to use a top dressing of gravel or chippings, now is the time to add this. There are many advantages of a top dressing. The most important to a busy gardener is that it will inhibit weed growth and help prevent moisture loss. This means maintenance of this type of rock garden will be minimal. Other advantages include better drainage and the prevention of soil compaction or slippage during heavy rain-

Cast cement statuary is inexpensive at garden outlets that offer pieces for sale.

fall. Providing the gravel or chippings selected are very similar in color and texture to the rock work it will blend together better than bare earth. Despite knowing all this and agreeing with it in principle, personally I hate to see this sort of barren rock and gravel combination. I know it is very fashionable now and I will probably be hated by the 'trendy' set for saying it, but I think it looks too sterile and uncompromising.

The choice of plants for your rock garden is huge and there is simply not enough room in this book to run through a comprehensive list of plants for a rockery. Many garden centers have large displays of alpines and each one should be labeled with the height, spread, flowering

Japanese long waterfall in which every rock has a designated location.

period and conditions they require. Apart from checking this information out, only select plants which have healthy compact foliage with no signs of weak straggly growth or yellowing of the leaves. Steer clear of any plant which has signs of attack by pests or diseases and try to buy young vigorous stock rather than big plants which may have more trouble adapting to your growing conditions.

A closeup of the large igneous (hard) rocks suitable for rockery around a water garden's edge.

FISH

Most people think of Goldfish and Koi when they think of fish for their pond but there are many more species which can be included. Some of these will be of definite benefit to the pond because they are good scavengers or will add to its beauty in some way. Others which are regularly offered for sale are not suitable for a garden pond and should not really be sold to the unsuspecting public.

Apart from choosing the right species for your pond, it is best to select healthy fish and to quarantine them in an aquarium for two weeks before they are introduced. Many shops simply acclimate their fish to the local water conditions. Given the fast turnover of fish required by a trade outlet, proper quarantining often becomes a luxury for sellers.

When buying new fish, take a close look at them and make sure their fins are well spread and free from damage. Small splits or nicks are not a problem providing they are clean and have no sign of fungus. Any fish with body damage should be avoided at all costs and it is worth checking to see that they have both eyes. Watch them for a while to make sure they are swimming well and appear to be active and healthy. Have a good look around to make sure there are no dead bodies in the tank or pond and if you are buying fish from a pond have a good look at them from the side when they are in the plastic bag.

When transporting fish make sure they are caught just before you are leaving the shop

fish

and try to go straight home. If you have to stop on the way home keep the fish with you if it is a hot day. Leaving the bags in a closed-up car on a hot day will cause the water temperature to shoot up very rapidly and can kill the fish.

When you arrive home open the top of each bag and float them in the quarantine tank or pond. After half an hour pour about a quarter of the water out and refill with tank water. Repeat this half an hour later and leave them for another half an hour after which they can be gently tipped out. Repeat the process when transferring the fish from your quarantine tank or pond into the main pond. This time a bucket containing the fish can be used but make sure you keep an eye on it. Cats find it much easier catching fish in a bucket than in the pond and you could find yourself supplying the local feline population with a free meal instead of stocking your pond. The following is a list of the more commonly found species of pond fish.

CATFISH

Catfish of various types are often offered for sale in garden centers and aquarium shops. These are usually sold as scavengers which will keep the pond clean. In fact most species do not grub around the substrate hunting out bits of uneaten food but are active nocturnal predators which will eat anything they can get into their very large mouths. Two common species you see offered for sale are Channel Cats (genus *Ictalurus*) which grow to 3 feet or more in length and (in the United Kingdom) the potentially huge Wels Catfish which may grow to 9 feet.

Ictalurus punctatus, a native American catfish used as a food fish, a game fish and a pond fish.

Photo by G. Parvis, Arkansas Fish and Game Bureau.

GOLDFISH

This is far and away the most widely kept fish in the world and justly deserving of its popularity. The Goldfish has been kept as an ornamen-

Photo by Fred Rosenzweig.

The shubunkin goldfish is suitable for the garden pond.

tal fish for thousands of years and through selective breeding has been changed beyond recognition. The wild form is a dull, brassy brown color and all baby goldfish start off this color. They do not develop their adult coloration until they are several months old, but despite thousands of years of selection, some fish from every brood still stay the wild color all their lives.

As you would expect over such a long period of time many different varieties of goldfish have been developed. Not all of these are hardy enough to be kept out in a pond all year round. This is particularly true of the northern United States and Canada. Ask your aquarium pet shop owner which Goldfish he recommends for your pond.

KOI

Koi are becoming increasingly popular but can only be kept in a large filtered pond because they produce large quantities of waste matter and love to munch on aquatic plants. It is possible to spend huge amounts of money on large Koi, but these animals grow very quickly and will reach the same size in only a year or two. It is, therefore, a much better idea to buy small fish and grow them up yourself. This way they will become accustomed to your conditions better and will become hand tame. Large older fish often remain nervous all their lives and can come down with disease more easily because of the stress caused by the move. Maximum size for Koi is about 30 inches. There are about eighteen recognized color varieties and many books written about Koi. These books are sold in most pet shops.

The basic book for koi lovers is Axelrod's KOI VARIETIES. Dr. Herbert Axelrod was the first one to import koi from Japan to the USA and UK in the late 1950's.

Photo by Michael Gilroy.

Colorful koi are, perhaps, the best fish for the garden pond.

OTHER ANIMALS

There are a whole range of other animals which can be introduced into a garden pond. I have always had a group of frogs and toads which have frequented my ponds. These eat slugs, snails and harmful insects so are a welcome addition to the wildlife living in my garden. I initially established them in each new garden by taking spawn from someone else's pond (not from the wild) and hatching out the tadpoles in a small pond or old tin tub. A large clump of oxygenating plants was placed in the container with the spawn and the tadpoles fed on this when they hatched out. Later a little flake food was added to their diet. Eventually they turned into little frogs and hopped away. About three years later a few returned to breed in my pond. The old wives' tale of frogs grabbing fish and killing them is something I have never seen and doubt ever really happens.

Newts and salamanders are other amphibians which can be established in a pond. These also feed on slugs, snails and insect life so are great assets in a garden. In the past I introduced adult newts to my ponds and established a breeding group this way but when I moved into my present home a breeding colony of Great Crested Newts lived in a natural pond just behind my garden. When the farmer decided to fill this in I dug my pond and the newts moved across of their own accord.

Dragonflies add a wonderful dimension to the pond during the summer months but their larvae are eaten by many fish and they may be a rare visitor to your pond. Other insects such as butterflies can be encouraged to your pond by growing the right sort of plants near it. *Buddleia* is one of the best for this and mine is positively covered with butterflies fluttering from bloom to bloom. Lavender is another useful plant in this respect and bees will swarm round this as well.

Here it is...the final result of an effort of love...the garden pond in the spring of the year!

There is a tremendous range of insects which turn up in and around a pond. One of the most harmful is the Great Diving Beetle. These beetles grow nearly two inches long and are dangerous predators which suck the juices out of fish and other soft-bodied animals. Fortunately they have to breathe atmospheric air and surface from time to time to do so. They can then be netted out and destroyed. Other insect pests include the Water Lily Beetle. These are small brown beetles which live on the top of water lily leaves. They and their gray grubs cut channels in the lily leaves and can cause great damage. To eradicate them simply submerge the lily leaves in water for a few days. This can be done either by holding the leaves under the surface with a wire mesh or by raising the water level. Either way the beetles and their larvae end up a tasty meal for the fish.

Photo by MP&C Piednoir.